FIVE RIGHTS

FIVE RIGHTS
"MEDICATION FOR YOUR SOUL"

Karen Deadwyler

Copyright © January 2010 by Karen Deadwyler

Published by
Godly Pleasures Inc.
North Massapequa, NY 11758
Www.godlypleasures.org

All rights reserved. No part of this publication may be reproduced, stored in a retrieval system or transmitted, in any form, or by any means, electronic, mechanical, recorded, photocopied, or otherwise, without the prior permission of the copyright owner, except by a reviewer who may quote brief passages in a review.

All Bible verses are from the Holy Bible KJV.

Cover Design By Apostle Karen Deadwyler

Printed in the United States of America

ISBN 978-0-9802390-1-0

Contents

Dedications 9
Acknowledgements 11
Foreword by Apostle Ronnie Deadwyler 15
Foreword by Jr. Chief Apostle Quester McKnight 17
Foreword by Apostle A. R. Kindle Jr. 19
About the Author, Karen Deadwyler 21
You Have the Right To Pray 25

Introduction 27
    You Have The Right 27
    Preface from the Lord 29

Chapter One: **He who sits at the Right Hand of the Father** .. 31
    His Birth 32
    Life 33
    Death (Burial) 35
    Resurrection (Power) 37
    Ascension 38

Chapter Two: **The Right Person** 41
    The Right Image of Christ 42
    The Body 43
    The Church as the Body 45

The Soul	45
The Emotions	46
Emotions built on sight	47
Emotions built on hearing	47
The Intellect	49
The Carnal Mind	50
My Spiritual Testimony	51
The Will	53
The Right Personality	54
Obedience	56
The Right Betrayer	57
A Right Heart: A Servant Heart	58
Forgiving Heart	60
The Right Call	61
Fivefold Ministry	62
The Right to Bind and Loose	64
The Right to Lift	65

Chapter Three: **The Right Medication (The Word)** 67

Bread from Heaven	69
Lighted Word	71
Corrective Word	75
Spoken Word	78

Chapter Four: **The Right Time** 81

You have the right to be in Gods timing!	81
Salvation Time	83
Watch and Pray	84

It is not time yet 85
In the Midst of Your Waiting Whatever He Says Do........... 86
The Appointed Time /Vision Time.. 87
Comforter 89
Eternity Time 90
At no time do we ever entertain the devil!............................. 91

Chapter Five: **The Right Dose (Faith and the Anointing)** 93
How do we Get Faith? 95
Levels of Faith... 96
Faith and the Anointing... 99

Chapter Six: **The Right Route** 103
Wounded and Rejected... 104
Crucified with Him 107
Count the Cost.. 109
Self-Denial... 112
Open and Shut Doors 114
Light Walking... 116
Ordered Steps.. 119
The Wrong Route... 121
Don't Become a Castaway.. 122
The Author and Finisher 124

Chapter Seven: **Medication for your Soul** 127
Rewards for Your Work.. 128
Learning by Afflictions 129
Hurt is Worth... 132

Persecuted for Righteousness Sake 134
Integrity and Trust 136
Do the Right Thing 137
Spiritual Maturity vs. Spiritual Immaturity 138
Doing It by The Spirit 139
When God Says "Yes" 141
Take it by Force 143
Warring in The Spirit 143
My Merry Heart 145
Medication to my Soul 146
Planted by the Water 148

Bibliography 151

DEDICATIONS

THIS book is dedicated to my cousin Barry Antley who left us suddenly this year to go be with the Father…We love you Beezo see you when I get there…

To my long time friend Rosita Lee this one is also for you as you battled a yearlong illness but God gave you victory over it all…

To the five most important people in my life

To the Most High God Jesus Christ who is my life, my strength, and my all and all. It is He that made it possible for me to write this book.

To my parents Deacon Clarence and Evangelist Pauline Owens I love you and I could never have come this far without your love and support. You're the best parents I could have ever asked for. God out did Himself with you two.

To my Husband Apostle Ronnie Deadwyler I will say the same thing I always say, "Love Does Truly Conquer All." Twenty-two years of marriage and counting and you are still my best friend and my all and all. I Love you for who you are and all you do. May the Lord continue to bless you for your faithfulness! God out did himself again this time in the husband category.

To my one and only sister; Evangelist Denise Owens: I call her my better half because her love for me always makes me strive to do better. I love you and thanks for always supporting me and loving me as your little sis. Once again God out did himself by giving me such a great and awesome big sister.

To all my friends and family that I cannot name one by one I love you all…

Acknowledgements

TO these three Apostles who have brought a New Greater Glory in my life…

To my Senior Pastor Apostle Ronnie Deadwyler you make it easy for me to be who God called me to be. I not only love you because you're my husband but because when it comes to Christ you are truly a walking example of a true servant.

To my Overseer Jr. Chief Apostle Quester McKnight… WOW…where do I start? You have been a great example of a true woman of God. I am truly glad you introduced me to a new realm of Gods Glory that has taken our ministry and our personal and spiritual lives to another dimension in Christ. You have been a true spiritual mother, mentor, and friend in the Gospel and in the natural. Thanks for all you have done in my life as well as in the lives of Glory Temple Ministries. Blessing to the New Jerusalem Family!

To Apostle A.R. Kindle Jr. and Lady Kindle: What can I say God has done some miraculous things in our spiritual and natural life? You two have become new friends and I thank God for meeting you. To the Apostle thanks for recognizing the call and anointing to elevate me to my next level in God or shall I say dimension. Blessings to the Greater Gethsemane Family!

To all my spiritual Fathers and Mothers in the Gospel thanks for everything that you have imparted into my life.

To my best friend from childhood, Prophetess Gio Allen: thanks for your help, friendship, covenant sisterhood, and spiritual covering that got me through a lot of the mess. Your intercessory prayers were priceless and I thank God for your spiritual discernment to recognize that I needed them.

To Glory Temple Ministries thanks for all you do to push me into my destiny and make the vision come to pass. I love you all and I thank God for each and every one of you individually and collectively.

To all the Willing Women of Worship Fellowship & Word in Action Intercessory Prayer Group: this is our fourth year and look how far God has brought us. Thanks for the prayers and the support when I needed it the most.

To the Montgomery Family (M.I.T. Larry, Pastor-Elect Joy & Prophetess April): Thanks for everything you have done and for the friendship and support in the natural and in the spiritual. To the Publisher: thanks for the open doors to be a columnist in the Community Journal and an Associate Editor of the Gospel News

Journal. May the Lord bless you for your obedience and give you all the desires of your heart…

Special thanks to Prophetess April Montgomery: who has become a great armor bearer and a wonderful spiritual daughter I really appreciate all you do.

To my Men-tee & Pastor-Elect Yolanda Grubbs: May God continue to use me to take you to your next dimension in God. I am thankful for what the Lord is doing in our lives as He elevates us in the spirit and the natural. Thanks for the marketing skills that God uses for you to promote my God-given talents.

Foreword by Apostle Ronnie Deadwyler

"The Father"

Grace, Mercy, and Peace from God our Father and Jesus Christ our Lord!

GOD has blessed me with a dynamic, energetic, and ever soaring eagle that can get in God's Glory and bring revelation back and write it; so she can share it all with everyone that will listen, read, and receive that which she has transcribed on paper. Her prophetic/apostolic scribe anointing makes you say wow to yourself for she makes the word of God real and alive. She is truly a gift from God. Words cannot describe my love for her and all the things she does in everyone's life. Her life is an open book that is available to all and the heart of her books is Jesus Christ. For He is the Way, the Truth, and the Life!

I have seen, heard, and witnessed this disciple of Jesus Christ Karen Deadwyler going forth, writing, teaching, and preaching the Gospel of our Lord and Savior Jesus Christ everywhere with the Lord working in her and confirming the word with signs following. Her first book "His Miraculous Way" has blessed so many lives and this second book the "Five Rights Medication for your Soul" is a covenant that God has placed in the heart of Apostle Karen Deadwyler. In this book Apostle Karen speaks life back into the Body of Christ from the experience that she endured during her spiritual walk.

The world and the church have a tendency to limit and bind you up if they do not understand your gift or spiritual walk that Christ has ordained for you. This book lets you know that Gods word is not to bind you but to liberate you and set the captive free. This book allows you to know that "Whom the Son (Jesus Christ) sets free is free indeed."

Through the mighty work of the Holy Spirit in the life of this Anointed Apostle we learn that even in death we can find life through Jesus Christ Rights.

With Love from Your Husband and Senior Pastor
Apostle Ronnie Deadwyler
Senior Pastor/ Glory Temple Ministries
North Massapequa, New York

Foreword by Jr. Chief Apostle Quester McKnight

"The Holy Spirit"

To God be the Glory for the things He has yet done, is doing, and about to do in Apostle Karen Deadwyler's life. It is a privilege and an honor to be one of the ones chosen to write this foreword for this Greatness that is being presented to the Body of Christ. The Greatness of this release of the book the "Five Rights Medication for your Soul" and the Greatness of the release of the Apostolic Mandate that is on Apostle Karen Deadwyler.

Who can tell you better of your rights in the Kingdom? Apostle Karen is allowing us to know just as there are patients' rights in the natural hospital; we also have servant's rights in the spiritual hospital. We need this spiritual medication for our souls to survive and make it to the end. She speaks about not allowing ourselves to become sick, delay our healing, or put ourselves at risk to die from the church due to the fact we did not know we had servants' rights in the Kingdom.

Apostle Karen Deadwyler has reached into the depths of her soul to write this book. A book to inform the Christian and non-Christian, how to survive after being administered the wrong medication. She's informing us we have a right to overcome spiritual and physical sickness and death. It is never too late to get the right medication for your soul to live again. Know your rights and know your five rights in the Kingdom. You will survive and get to your destiny in God. Know you are the right servant for the job, getting the right medication; being administered the right dose, at the right time so you can go into the right direction with the Father.

This book is a must read especially for the Body of Christ so we can stop going in the wrong direction. If you feel you are doing right, still read it to make sure. If you are ready to be the right servant, to get your right medication, the right dose, at the right time so you can get to your right destiny in the right timing of God.

I challenge you, but most of all I encourage you to read it, apply it, walk in it, and be it. It is the right medication for your soul. You have the right to know your rights....

Love Jr. Chief Apostle Quester McKnight
Senior Pastor / New Jerusalem Healing and Deliverance Ministries
Jr. Chief Apostle to Chief Apostle/Overseer Apostle Jessie Edrington
Greater Ministries of Blessings Liberated Assemblies Inc.

Foreword by Apostle A. R. Kindle Jr.

"The Son"

In the natural when you go to the doctor's office, there is posted patients' Bill of Rights. These rights guarantee you as a patient prompt courteous professional care and service. Those rights are placed there to make you feel confident about choosing that practice to service your health needs and concerns. In the spiritual you are also guaranteed spiritual medical rights. You have the right to salvation. You have the right to go to the Father through the blood of the Son, Jesus Christ. You have the right to prosper and be in good health even as you prosper. Since we have these rights, why don't we use them? Why don't we access our privileges to those Spiritual Rights?

Medication doesn't have any effect if it is not taken according to the prescribed dosage and the amount of times per day. By not following the doctor's directions for the medication, it only delays your recovery and further aggravates your condition. Fear of the side effects also causes us not to start our medication regime. Although some side effects can be positive and yield some good results.

The Bible is clear about our current state of Spiritual health. God has not given us the spirit of fear but of love, power, and a sound mind. Healing is not only a process but also a mind set, a spiritual transformation. Paul said Let this mind be in you that was in Christ Jesus (Philippians 2:5). He recognized that in order for one to change, it starts with one's mind. Your healing, your deliverance, your break through is only Five Rights away.

Is there no balm in Gilead; is there no physician there? Why then is not the health of the daughter of my people recovered? (Jeremiah 8:22). You can be healed and recover if you know your spiritual medical rights. Get to know the Five Rights "Medication for your Soul for your blessings is just" Five Rights" away!

Grace and Peace
Apostle A. R. Kindle Jr.
Pastor /Greater Gethsemane Oil of Anointing F.B.H. Church Yonkers, New York

About the Author

Karen Deadwyler

I was born in Brooklyn, N.Y. When I was seven my parents moved to Baldwin, Long Island where my sister and I were raised. I am a graduate of Uniondale High School and BOCES where I received my nursing training while in my junior and senior years of high school. I was licensed as an L.P.N. in 1982 and have twenty-five years experience in all areas of nursing.

I desire to return to college for a BA in business administration and finance so that I may become savvier in running the businesses that God has given me. Currently I own a business called Godly Pleasures Inc. (www.godlypleasures.org). I am a graduate of the House of Refuge Bible Institute achieving a Bachelor of Theology/ Major in Christian Education from International Theological Seminary of California.

In addition, God has inspired me to write several prayers, the most popular ones being "A Prayer for Strength" and "As We Kneel at the Foot of the Cross," I also had the honor and privilege of self-publishing my first book in 2008 called "His Miraculous Way" Which you can find on my website as well as on Barnes

& Noble's or Amazon .com. I also write a weekly column titled "Life Changing Words" in the Long Island Community Journal as well as I am an Associate Editor of the Gospel News Journal. I know that I have been called to inspire and encourage new authors in the Body of Christ to write for the Kingdom of God. I am also called to assist them in getting their writings and/or books self-published.

I am married to my best friend for twenty-two years and counting. We Pastor the church Glory Temple Ministries Inc. together where he is the Senior Pastor and I am The Pastor/Prophetess of the house. We both walk in the apostolic anointing and are Apostles under the leadership and covering of Jr. Chief Apostle Quester McKnight of New Jerusalem Healing and Deliverance Ministries Inc. in Brooklyn, N.Y.

My goals are to open up an abuse shelter for women and children and a clinic to help teenage mothers and women out of prison. I know I have been called to preach the Gospel across the nation, to do conferences and seminars, and to open up soup kitchens as well as homeless shelters. As Jesus said, "That if I do it for the least of them you have done it to me."

Now that I have moved into my next dimension and realm in God, I decided to go forth in all areas in which God has called me, and so I desire to learn all that I can while taking all the steps necessary in ministry to perfect the calling that is on my life. I have not only been called but also chosen to do great things for the

Kingdom. My prayer is that I will complete everything that God has entrusted to me in an orderly and excellent manner until He calls me to Glory.

Grace and Peace with Love

YOU HAVE THE RIGHT TO PRAY

Father in the precious name of Jesus
I thank You for giving me the right, to write
this book unto your people.

Let it be nourishment to their spirit
and medication to their souls.

Let them learn that in You there is no failure
and certainly no wrong way of doing things.
Everything about You Lord is Righteous and Holy.

Let this book exemplify who You
are according to Your word.

Let us gain wisdom, knowledge, and understanding
of the Five Rights that You have
entrusted to me your servant to write.

And above all things let everyone realize that reads
this book that we have the right to
Pray!!!!

AMEN AMEN AMEN
Karen Deadwyler
Copyright©2009

Introduction

You Have The Right

"Therefore I esteem all thy precepts concerning all things to be right; and I hate every false way".

Psalms 119:128 KJV

WE must understand that all of Gods statues, commands, and laws are right. For God is Righteous and He hates any other way.

This book is written to inform you of your rights. I call them the five rights and when done according to God's will and His ways, it will and shall become medication to your Soul. In writing this book the Lord lead me down the path of a natural and spiritual comparison of what I call the dispensing rules of medication. As a nurse when we talk about medication and learning how to administer it correctly we are taught the **five rights.**

In the natural or in a medical setting the five rights would be the right patient, the right medication, the right dose, the right time and the right route. This would be the ideal situation and the only proper way to administer medication that the doctor has ordered for a particular person. Given any other way would be considered an error even if by chance you happen to get all five rights. Why? Because of your disobedience to the rules or the method has not been followed according to the plans of the Professor and/or Teacher. You must check all five and be absolutely sure that they are right before you ever administer any medication.

Now in the spiritual realm you as a Christian and/or non-Christian have the same five rights just as the patients have. You have the Right to the Father through the Son, you have the right to be medicated by The Word, you have the right to a dose of the anointing and faith, you have the right to be in Gods timing, and you have the right to take Gods route through the Cross to your purpose, plan and destiny…

The reason why you must be taught this is because if any of the five rights are wrong, it can cause sickness, delay your healing, put you at risk for death or maybe even kill you. This works the same way in the spirit. What am I trying to say? That if you miss out on one of the five rights during your walk with Christ the same thing can and will happen. You will be walking in *error* and there is a price to pay.

However hopefully there will come a time in every Christian's life when all five will line up. When this happens you will have walked into the plan, purpose, and destiny that Christ has for your life and then it becomes like medication to your soul…

Preface from the Lord

When I began to seek the Father for wisdom and guidance as to where to start with this book the Lord said start with "*The Son*" who is seated at the right hand of the Father and tell the people How He got there. For you can't assume that all of your reader's will be knowledgeable of the Bible so you must act and write this book like as if they have never picked one up. So your first job as prophetic scribe is to tell your readers about *"The Son of God, Christ, the Son of the Blessed."* Since the title of this book is the five rights. I decided to tell you about the five most important and crucial steps that Jesus took in His life. For it is through His life we received the right to the Father and the rights to the Kingdom of Heaven.

Chapter One

He who sits at the Right Hand of the Father

> "Art thou the Christ? Tell us. And he said unto them, If I tell you, ye will not believe: And if I also ask you, ye will not answer me, nor let me go. Hereafter shall the Son of man sit on the right hand of the power of God."
>
> (Luke 22:67-69 KJV)

> "But he held his peace, and answered nothing. Again the high priest asked him, and said unto him, Art thou the Christ, the Son of the Blessed? And Jesus said, I am: and ye shall see the Son of man sitting on the right hand of power, and coming in the clouds of heaven."
>
> (Mark 14:61-62 KJV)

AT the beginning of every chapter and book you must always lay a good solid foundation. Here I will lay the foundation of Jesus and His Birth, Life, Death (Burial), Resurrection (Power), and Ascension. This way you will have a clear understanding of who Jesus Christ is and how you can walk in victory through Him.

It will also help you to understand the five rights as I lay them out for you with scripture backup.

HIS BIRTH

"Now the birth of Jesus Christ was on this wise: When as his mother Mary was espoused to Joseph, before they came together, she was found with child of the Holy Ghost."

(Matthew 1:18 KJV)

"And the angel answered and said unto her, The Holy Ghost shall come upon thee, and the power of the Highest shall overshadow thee: therefore also that holy thing which shall be born of thee shall be called the Son of God."

(Luke 1:35 KJV)

First let's look at why Jesus had to be born because man had fallen into the hands of Satan because of his disobedience to the word of God. We no longer had fellowship with God for Satan had deceived man into believing that God was trying to keep him from something good; when the Lord was trying to keep man from evil. So God had to come down to earth in human form and redeem man from "The Fall." His plan was to use a virgin girl called Mary who would birth Jesus Christ *"The Anointed One"*. The Holy Spirit had impregnated her for it could not be the seed of a man but it must be from God. For man had been tainted and no longer was sinless. Now because of Adam's disobedience to God all humankind was born in sin and shaped in iniquity. "For as by one man's disobedience many were made sinners, so by the obedience of one shall many be made righteous." (Rom 5:19 KJV)

So now that we have learned why Jesus must be born and how He has entered into the world in human form. Yet He was all man and all God. His deity had not been changed or compromised. I will never understand how God managed to put all of his infinite power, wisdom, and holiness in the body of a babe. However that is why He is called God because He is able to do all things and has no limits or limitations. He is Alpha and Omega. He is the beginning and the end at the same time. For He is God at all times but yet, He is born of the flesh as a baby and must live life just as we do (yet sinless) and go through the process of growing up. Picture that "How does God really grow up? That in itself is a mystery and food for thought…

LIFE

"But he turned, and rebuked them, and said, Ye know not what manner of spirit ye are of.
For the Son of man is not come to destroy men's lives, but to save them. And they went to another village."
(Luke 9:55-56 KJV)

Jesus grew up and went through all the stages of growth and development as we all did. He never used his power to change any part of the growing process. He was never spoken of as having done any supernatural or miraculous healing as a child or young adult. However we do find out that about the age of twelve He had exhibited Godly wisdom for He was in the synagogue teaching. *"And when he was twelve years old, they went up to Jerusalem after the custom of the feast. And when they had fulfilled the days, as they returned, the child Jesus tarried behind in Jerusalem; and Joseph and his mother knew not of it. But they, supposing him to have been in the company, went a day's journey; and they sought him among their kinsfolk and acquaintance. And when they found him not, they turned back again to Jerusalem, seeking him. And it came to pass, that after three days they found him in the temple, sitting in the midst of the doctors, both hearing them, and asking them questions. And all that heard him were astonished at his understanding and answers. And when they saw him, they were amazed: and his mother said unto him, Son, why hast thou thus dealt with us? behold, thy father and I have sought thee sorrowing. And he said unto them, How is it that ye sought me? Wist ye not that I must be about my Father's business? And they understood not the saying which he spake unto them. And he went down with them, and came to Nazareth, and was subject unto them: but his mother kept all these sayings in her heart. And Jesus increased in wisdom and stature, and in favour with God and man."* (Luke 2:42-52 KJV)

We know that He was trained by his earthly father Joseph to be a carpenter. However Jesus doesn't really start His ministry until approximately thirty years old when He is baptized by His forerunner John "The Baptist". *"Now when all the people were baptized, it came to pass, that Jesus also being baptized, and praying, the heaven was opened, And the Holy Ghost descended in a bodily shape like a dove upon him, and a voice came from heaven, which* said, Thou art my beloved Son; in thee I am well pleased. And Jesus himself began to be about thirty years of age, being (as was supposed) the son of Joseph, which was the son of Heli." (Luke 3:21-23 KJV)

John was called to prepare "The Way" and Jesus would ultimately proclaim, "I am The Way." *"For this is he, of whom it is written, Behold, I send my messenger before thy face, which shall prepare thy way before thee. Verily I say unto you, Among them that are born of women there hath not risen a greater than John the Baptist: notwithstanding he that is least in the kingdom of heaven is greater than he." (Mat 11:10-11 KJV)* For Jesus ministry lasted about three years as He went around healing the sick, raising the dead, and preaching to the multitudes. Exhibiting great wisdom and power, which would expose Him to the world and create jealousy, envy, and strife among those who could not understand His ways or His mission? For He said I would come as a King and reign forever. Yet death must come for Him so freedom and reconciliation can come for us. But if death comes for *Christ: The King* how can He reign forever?

DEATH (BURIAL)

"And the sun was darkened, and the veil of the temple was rent in the midst. And when Jesus had cried with a loud voice, he said, Father, into thy hands I commend my spirit: and having said thus, he gave up the ghost."

(Luke 23:45-46 KJV)

For death was inevitable because that was Gods purpose to

come and die for us all. Jesus must pay the price for the entire mankind once and for all. *"For if by one man's offence death reigned by one; much more they which receive abundance of grace and of the gift of righteousness shall reign in life by one, Jesus Christ." (Rom 5:17 KJV)* For the law would be fulfilled for He had lived His life holy and sinless. And now we would be free to live life by grace (unmerited favor) through faith. Yet He must die a horrible and shameful death being crucified on the Cross. He would become the *Suffering Servant* for all; carrying every sin possible that would ever exist now and forever more. Being beaten, bruised, despised, and rejected by man for the sake of doing good. How many of us have gone through this same kind of treatment? Yet even through all of this there was one thing that we must not forget before the grave and burial comes.

We must remember it was all for the Blood **for without the shedding of Blood there is no remission of sin**. So now that we have captured it all: His purpose, the law, the beaten, the suffering, and the Blood we can bury Jesus. His words were in three days I will resurrect this temple. *"Saying, The Son of man must be delivered into the hands of sinful men, and be crucified, and the third day rise again, And they remembered his words," (Luke 24:7-8 KJV)* Surely no one knew or understood that He meant His body would be resurrected and not a building made by hands…Hallelujah!

For remember Jesus said it is finished and He gave up the Ghost for the words of our Lord was that no one takes His life but that He laid it down for the sheep. "As the Father knoweth me, even so know I the Father: and I lay down my life for the sheep. And other sheep I have, which are not of this fold: them also I must bring, and they shall hear my voice; and there shall be one fold, and one shepherd. Therefore doth my Father love me, because I lay down my life, that I might take it again? No man taketh it from me, but I lay it down of myself. I have power to lay it down, and I have power to take it again. This commandment have I received of my Father." (John 10:15-18 KJV)

RESURRECTION (POWER)

"And it came to pass, as they were much perplexed thereabout, behold, two men stood by them in shining garments: And as they were afraid, and bowed down their faces to the earth, they said unto them, Why seek ye the living among the dead? He is not here, but is risen: remember how he spake unto you when he was yet in Galilee,"

(Luke 24:4-6KJV)

Oh death where is thy sting oh grave where is thy victory for the King of Glory has risen. He is not dead…He has risen for the grave could not hold Him and Satan had not conquered Him. For God has done the ultimate miracle of them all. Jesus has risen from the grave never to die again. Though scientist can't explain it and atheist don't believe in it. If the Power of God has ever touched you no one will ever have to convince you that God is real and His Power, which is the Holy Spirit, can raise you from the dead. I know about His resurrection Power first hand for I should be dead but I am alive so I can be a living epistle as well as a living testimony.

ASCENSION

"And he led them out as far as to Bethany, and he lifted up his hands, and blessed them. And it came to pass, while he blessed them, he was parted from them, and carried up into heaven."
(Luke 24:50-51 KJV)

It is now ascension time but before Christ leaves it is imperative that He leaves us instructions. First we must understand that all O.T prophecy about the coming Messiah has just been fulfilled. For the Lord has redeemed His people from the hands of Satan and brought them back into reconciliation (fellowship) with Him. Now we no longer have to live by the Law but there is a new covenant that is greater than the previous one. "But now hath he obtained a more excellent ministry, by how much also he is the mediator of a better covenant, which was established upon better promises. For if that first covenant had been faultless, then should no place have been sought for the second." (Hebrews 8:6-7 KJV) We no longer need animal sacrifices for repentance to go to the Father in prayer but we now can enter into Gods presence for ourselves. We no longer needed any priest to go into the Holy of Holies and stand in the gap for us. "Who is he that condemneth? It is Christ that died, yea rather, that is risen again, who is even at the right hand of God, who also maketh intercession for us." (Romans 8:34 KJV) Now Jesus has become our great intercessor and our High Priest.

To be seated at the Right hand side of the *FATHER IS A PLACE OF HONOR but YET HUMILITY.* For Christ had to be born, live as a servant, shed his blood, be hung on a cross, and die a horrible and shameful death, to get to that seat (right hand of the Father). He had to take the death walk just as we do. We must die to the flesh to live for Christ. Though many want to get to that place of high honor but Christ asked a question and so I present it to the readers who desire these high positions of honor. Can you drink from the cup that Christ did? Of course not but we do have our own cups to drink from and at times it can be sweet but others it can be Bitter…To whom much is given remember much is required. The greater the call the greater the test!

Now that Christ has taken His seat at the right hand of the Father He gives us the right to fulfill life's plan, purpose, and destiny. Through Him we have the right to the five rights as we enter into the next chapter of this book as well as the next chapter of our life. Jesus gave us the right to live and live more abundantly why not take Him up on it. For you have the Right!!!!

You have the Right to the Father through the Son!
As the father has sent me so I send you.
So my job as the writer is to lift Him up and He will draw all the reader's to thee….

Chapter Two

The Right Person

"For in him we live, and move, and have our being; as certain also of your own poets have said, For we are also his offspring. Forasmuch then as we are the offspring of God, we ought not to think that the Godhead is like unto gold, or silver, or stone, graven by art and man's device. And the times of this ignorance God winked at; but now commandeth all men every where to repent:"

(Acts 17:28-30 KJV)

AS Christians and children of the Most High God everything that we do and/or exhibit should line up with the Word of God. We do not have to wonder about whom to follow for we have a perfect example in Christ. For truly it is in Him that we live , move and have our being. Our lives should be centered on Him. I can guarantee you if you put Him first He will handle all things pertaining to your life and handle them well.

We can put our focus solely on God because in Him is the source of all life. He is the creator, sustainer, and provider of everything. Nothing was made without Him. Many of us take for granted life in general until our fiery trials show up. It is then that we realize that we need God. It is at that time of suffering, pain, loss, hurt, discouragement, or depression that we find Jesus. It is then that we begin to recognize that He alone is the **right person** for the job. He is the only one who can meet all of our needs. Not just our spiritual needs but our physical, financial, emotional, and social needs as well. Jesus is the complete package in Him you find wholeness, holiness, and wholesomeness. However one of His greatest attributes is Righteousness!!!

In accordance with picking the right person let us look at Jesus.

THE RIGHT IMAGE OF CHRIST

*"And God said, Let us make man **in our image, after our likeness**: and let them have dominion over the fish of the sea, and over the fowl of the air, and over the cattle, and over all the earth, and over every creeping thing that creepeth upon the earth.*

So God created man in his own image, in the image of God created he him; male and female created he them."
(Genesis 1:26-27 KJV)

In the beginning when God created man. He created us in the image and likeness of Himself; meaning that we were created to be righteous and holy just as He is. We were also created as a triune being meaning (consisting of three parts) the body, the soul and the spirit. Just as God from the beginning consisted of the Father, the Son, and The Holy Spirit for if you read the word closely it says and I quote "Let us make man in **our** image, after **our** likeness." Showing you that from the beginning the Trinity existed (one God existing in three persons) and if you choose to argue the fact then know that the word **our** represents more than one. Now according to the Bible, which is the only infallible word of God, there is only one God, one Faith, and one Baptism. So for the atheist and the skeptics I then leave you with the question of who is our as I move on.... Now let us deal with the three parts of man, which we call a triune being.

The Body

First let us deal with the body, which are the flesh in the natural and the church in the spiritual. We will start with the flesh first. Let me ask you this question. What image does your body give off? A lot of times we judge a book by its cover instead of by the substance inside. We look through the natural eyes and assume many things about people that are not always necessarily true. Thank God that the Lord looks at the heart. *"But the LORD said unto Samuel, Look not on his countenance, or on the height of his stature; because I have refused him: for the LORD seeth not as man seeth; for man looketh on the outward appearance, but the LORD looketh on the heart." (1 Samuel 16:7 KJV)*

Our body can tell people many things for instance body mechanics are unspoken words. It can tell us how you feel physically and emotionally without you ever even opening your mouth. And let's not even talk about your eyes. For the scripture says the eyes are the windows to your soul when I look at your eyes what do they say? Will your eyes bless me or curse me, validate me or belittle me? These are the things that we do to make people feel ashamed, cause them to stumble in life, and maybe even fall. Many of our insecurity issues come from this very behavior. And I say ours because everyone is insecure about something for example some are insecure about there bodies others are insecure about their mind. Whatever the issue might be it is stemming from the way people respond and act towards you. We must watch being so harsh and so judgmental of people for the same measure that you judge people you will also be judged. *"Judge not, that ye be not judged. For with what judgment ye judge, ye shall be judged: and with what measure ye mete, it shall be measured to you again."* (Matthew 7:1-2 KJV)

We must understand that we live in a free country and all of us differ in many ways and for several different reasons. Nevertheless it is still not our job to judge one another, how about we just love one another, and let God do the rest. It is His image that we want to portray and it is through His spirit and His word that He will teach us how to present our bodies. In Romans 12:1 KJV it simply says *"I beseech you therefore, brethren, by the mercies of God, that ye present your bodies a living sacrifice, holy, acceptable unto God, which is your reasonable service."* Know that if you present your body correctly (holy and acceptable to God) then you will present the right image. You can and will be a living example of who Christ called you to be.

The Church as the Body

The church, which is the Body of Christ, also has an image to maintain for the non-believers as well as the believers. The church is for building up of the Kingdom and to help the Christians mature in the faith. Though we have multiple duties the main purpose of the church is to do the Great Commission (saving souls).

The Soul

"And be not conformed to this world: but be ye transformed by the renewing of your mind, that ye may prove what is that good, and acceptable, and perfect, will of God."
(Romans 12:2 KJV)

Our soul/mind consists of our emotions, intellect and our will. **The soul** refers to the animating and vital principle in human beings, credited with faculties of thought, action, and emotion and often conceived as an immaterial entity. **The mind** is the human consciousness that originates in the brain and is manifested esp. in thought, perception, emotion, will, memory, and imagination.

These two are close in proximity if not the same thing. There have been arguments back and forth about this issue whether the mind and soul are one. I am not going to argue this point I will just give to you what God has inspired me to say. Now when we talk about the mind/soul or conscious there are a few words we must define before we move on. We must define these three words (emotions, intellect, and will) so we can not only get wisdom, knowledge and understanding but be able to maintain it as well.

The emotions *refer to an intense mental state that arises subjectively rather than through conscious effort; the part of the consciousness that involves feelings and sensibility.*

The intellect *refers to the ability to learn and reason; the capacity of knowledge and understanding or the ability to think abstractly or profoundly.*

The will *refers to the mental faculty by which one deliberately chooses or decides upon a course of action.*

THE EMOTIONS

The emotions *refer to an intense mental state that arises subjectively rather than through conscious effort; the part of the consciousness that involves feelings and sensibility.*

Now this on the other hand has nothing to do with our faith but it will hinder your actions and cause you to doubt. The first thing that we must look at when it comes to emotions is *personal gain or desire*. And I say that first because if you begin to walk in emotions instead of intellect and/or faith the first thing we will fulfill or desire is our own selfish needs. We start to think of self-first and not Christ. This in itself can produce a world of trouble in the life of a Christian (a believer in Christ).

EMOTIONS BUILT ON SIGHT

For the scripture says that we are **to walk by faith and not by sight** however most of the times our emotions are built upon sight or on one of our five senses. We usually react according to what we see, hear, or feel and not on the true facts. The true facts according to the Bible say something completely different than what we may be seeing, hearing, or feeling. For example according to God and His word I am considered to be a prophetess but however to those who work with me in the natural or secular world I am a nurse. Which in reality I am both but you can only see one of those titles in the natural; the other one is not visible to the naked eye. I used this as an example so that you can realize that you must not get emotional about everything you see because looks can be deceiving. For when looking at me in the natural you couldn't see the whole picture you only saw part or shall I say a glimpse of whom I really am. This is why we must not let sight rule our emotions for it takes us off the path of faith and into our own imagination and that can be dangerous at times...

EMOTIONS BUILT ON HEARING

"Cease, my son, to hear the instruction that causeth to err from the words of knowledge"

(Proverbs 19:27 KJV)

And surely you cannot go by what you hear because everybody is not speaking the truth. There are people who speak solely on their emotions. If they like you they speak good things about you but if they don't like you or something about you they may speak bad things. So you must be careful who speaks to you and whose words you receive in your ear for sometimes a whispering spirit can be a dangerous thing. Many people have reacted badly on a lie and had to pay the price for their emotions instead of taking a moment to evaluate the truth. You must use your wisdom and knowledge when listening to anyone. *"A wise man will hear, and will increase learning; and a man of understanding shall attain unto wise counsels." (Proverbs 1:5 KJV)* We must first take into account the person who is speaking. Are they trustworthy and what does their character say about them? Do they have a history of speaking negative or falsely against someone? *"Bow down thine ear, and hear the words of the wise, and apply thine heart unto my knowledge." (Proverbs 22:17 KJV)*

Our emotions don't usually respond to our intellect it usually responds to our five senses.

This is one of the things that you find is running ramped in the church. Satan is using our five senses to make us spiritual schizophrenics. One day you're fine and the next day you are an emotional wreck for what someone has said or seen and then informed you. Let me remind you that emotions have nothing to do with our faith when used negatively against one another. We as Christians must ask God to mature us in our faith so that we won't be moved by emotions but grounded in faith through our spiritual intellect. Now let me close this section on emotions with this if there is no love (charity) all our work is in vain.

"Though I speak with the tongues of men and of angels, and have not charity, I am become as sounding brass, or a tinkling cymbal. And though I have the gift of prophecy, and understand all mysteries, and all knowledge; and though I have all faith, so that I could remove mountains, and have not charity, I am nothing. And though I bestow all my goods to feed the poor, and though I give my body to be burned, and have not charity, it profiteth me nothing."

(1 Corinthians 13:1-3 KJV)

For without love you cannot and will not exhibit the image of Christ. Man must not let his emotions take him out of the will of God. *"And now abideth faith, hope, charity, these three; but the greatest of these is charity." (1 Corinthians 13:13 KJV)*

THE INTELLECT

The intellect *refers to the ability to learn and reason; the capacity of knowledge and understanding or the ability to think abstractly or profoundly.* Now this on the other hand has nothing to do with our faith but it will hinder your actions and cause you to doubt.

When we look at the intellect of Jesus we certainly cannot be exactly like Him for He is omniscience but we strive to be naturally intellectual as well as spiritually intellectual. Natural intellect tells you how the world thinks and lives however spiritual intellect is based on the word of God and on your faith. For if we are to duplicate the image of Christ then we must learn His ways, thoughts, commands, and statues let alone His will. For we must renew our mind and begin to think like Christ as the scripture says *Let this mind be in you that is also in Christ Jesus.* This simply means that it going to take work and faith to develop our spiritual intellect so that we can catapult our faith to become like Christ. See Jesus had no shadow of a doubt that if the Father spoke it that it was already done and just needed it to be manifested in the natural realm. When He spoke he got the attention of everyone and because He was wisdom in the flesh everything He spoke had to come to pass.

The Carnal Mind

A carnal mind means the mind of a natural thinker somebody who only thinks about worldly issues, whether they be good or bad thoughts. It is just things of the flesh meaning it have no spiritual connections or connotations. As much as we desire to be successful in all things a natural thinking mind can never understand spiritual (divine) things. See we have to look at the spiritual intellect to obtain some of the blessings and promises of God. Some blessings and promises we can only receive through faith. We must believe spiritually first to obtain anything naturally. For all things happen in the spirit realm first then it will manifest in the natural (world).

Just to give you a few examples so you can understand natural vs. spiritual a little better. Natural intellect says you only have a high school Diploma so you cannot obtain a job that will require a college degree. However your spiritual intellect will tell you that according to your faith mixed with the word of God and the favor of God I can obtain that job although naturally I don't have the qualifications. See your spiritual intellect takes you to another level that supersedes the worlds thinking. It also tells you God is Sovereign and if it is Gods will no one or nothing can change His Words or stop the plans that He has for your life.

My Spiritual Testimony

Another example I will use myself for instance. Naturally I have right femoral nerve damage, limited mobility yet constant pain and considered disabled. So my natural mind wants to give up and give in to this unfortunate mishap by doctors during a surgical procedure, which literally left me disabled. But God said no I shall give you the ability in your state of being to use your spiritual intellect and faith to push past your flesh into your promises. I shall not remove it but I shall renew your mind to walk with it. For as I have told the apostle Paul; I shall also tell you Karen "My Grace is sufficient for when you are weak I am yet strong." After a seven-year battle with chair and bed rest, lost of independence, lack of mobility, and the lost of a lawsuit. I am yet back because my spiritual intellect kept reminding me that Gods word outweighs whatever the body feels and whatever the carnal mind can think or imagine. Even when it doesn't make sense or even when it looks impossible to the naked eye Gods word outweighs it. See my spiritual intellect has taught me that with God all things are Possible. For it is through Christ that I receive the strength I need to overcome all things…

My last example of the natural vs. the spiritual intellect I will go a little deeper into my personal business. In the midst of all that I had been through prior to this I had just brought another house this time bigger and what we would call better. Meaning quite simply that most of my bills had increased and my mortgage itself had doubled. I was only in this new home two months before tragedy hit me and I was fighting for my life. In the midst of all this as I stated earlier I wand up being disabled meaning unable to work, not receiving disability (because the doctors would not admit they made mistakes and was negligent) and basically new bills and loss of money.

God made a promise to me that I would not lose anything and not one thing would be repossessed or cut off. Now there were some hard times and even sometimes when it really looked dim but God kept His promises. Every time when times would get hard and things would look impossible I had to rely on my spiritual intellect and remind myself what God had promised me. It wasn't always easy but one thing I know God was faithful and He kept His word. Now seven years later here I am telling you the story about how God kept me alive, kept His promises and how my spiritual intellect mixed with my faith kept me from losing my mind. See if I did not know Gods will for my life during this storm then I could not have persevere and made it through. This in itself should help you with our next topic...

The Will

The will *refers to the mental faculty by which one deliberately chooses or decides upon a course of action.* **This helps us to work our faith for we know faith without works is dead.**

When we look at the will there are two distinctive choices that we can make one is our will or the other is God's will. Naturally the better choice is always God's will, but ninety-nine percent of the time it goes against our will. Why? Because man's natural will (which are our own desires) want to please and pacify our flesh. However **God's will** naturally wants to follow the things of the spirit, which will please God. What's so wonderful about God is He gives you a choice and a chance to choose the correct way. He does not hound you or force you to do anything against your will.

See we serve a God who is Sovereign and knows all things past, present and future but yet allows us to choose some of the wrong ways, experience some hardships and dilemmas and stills grants us mercy and grace to get back on course and choose His will. God doesn't push you to do anything against your will but He will allow you to read, study, learn, and follow His ways and statues so that you can make sound and deliberate choices and actions.

For example when you look at a living will in the natural it is no good until the persons dies then it has power and the document supersedes anything or anyone's wishes that goes against what the deceased has granted. It is the same thing in the spiritual world once you die to your will (personal/fleshly desires) then God's will shall supersede yours and you will be the inherit of something much greater. You will now become an heir to God's throne, which will qualify you to receive all promises, and blessings that He has ordained in His word. *"For whom he did foreknow, he also did predestinate to be conformed to the **image of his Son**, that he might be the firstborn among many brethren. Moreover whom he did predestinate, them he also called: and whom he called, them he also justified: and whom he justified, them he also glorified. What shall we then say to these things? If God be for us, who can be against us?"* (Romans 8:29-31 KJV)

The Right Personality

"But when Jesus heard that, he said unto them, They that be whole need not a physician, but they that are sick. But go ye and learn what that meaneth, I will have mercy, and not sacrifice: for I am not come to call the righteous, but sinners to repentance."

(Matthew 9:12-13 KJV)

"When Jesus heard it, he saith unto them, They that are whole have no need of the physician, but they that are sick: I came not to call the righteous, but sinners to repentance."

(Mark 2:17 KJV)

Here we are still under the title of the Right person though our subtitle is the right personality. What is a personality and how can we determine if ours is right or wrong? Well according to the dictionary the word ***personality*** means the totality of qualities and traits, as of character or behavior, peculiar to a specific person; the pattern of collective character, behavioral, temperamental, emotional, and mental traits of a person; distinctive qualities of a person, esp. those distinguishing personal characteristics that make one socially appealing.

When we talk about being the right person the first thing that comes to mind is we must be in right standing with Christ. Which means our character must line up with His word. What does the word say about our character? Let's take a look at the word... Now when we look at the personality or character of Jesus then we can understand whom we are to mimic. His character is righteous, just; truth, peaceful and the epitome of love but yet sinless. Surely we can't be all those things by ourselves but He has sent the Holy Spirit to help you walk upright before Him. Yes none of us is perfect or shall I say mature in the faith but we must be striving to be like Jesus. We must lay down some of these bad habits and rude behavior that is hindering the Body of Christ from going forward.

How can we explain to a non-believer that you are nasty, rude and unruly and yet you are a Pastor? A Pastor or any of the fivefold ministry ought to be a representation of Jesus meaning we should be exhibiting the fruit of the Spirit. *"But the fruit of the Spirit is love, joy, peace, longsuffering, gentleness, goodness, faith, meekness, temperance: against such there is no law." (Galatians 5:22-23 KJV)* A Christian's character should lead people to Christ not in the opposite direction. We have to show them that living for Christ do make a difference in our lives, in our character and in our behavior. We dare not exhibit what the world does, for if we do then what difference are we making. *We must use our helper the Holy Spirit to discipline us so that our integrity can stand up to our titles.* Am I saying that we will be perfect Christians of course not; but what I am saying is honor what you believe in and most importantly honor the Lord!

OBEDIENCE

"And Samuel said, Hath the LORD as great delight in burnt offerings and sacrifices, as in obeying the voice of the LORD? Behold, to obey is better than sacrifice, and to hearken than the fat of rams. For rebellion is as the sin of witchcraft, and stubbornness is as iniquity and idolatry. Because thou hast rejected the word of the LORD, he hath also rejected thee from being king"

(1 Samuel 15:22-23 KJV)

I have heard this scripture quoted continuously wrong as I walk into my calling. It does not mean that you are to be enslaved to your leaders or any person for that matter. Listen if and I repeat this word again *if* your obedience to anyone or anything produces bondage it is not obedience to God's will. For the word of the Lord simply says, "Whom the Son set free is free indeed and where the spirit of the Lord is there is liberty."

Obedience is better than sacrifice means in a simplistic way that if you were obedient to the word of God from the beginning you will not have to take the trip back to the Cross-to repent for doing things out of the will and ways of God. So leaders honor your followers and let's not put our church in bondage but let them be free to do the will and the work of the Lord. Now however church let us get it right as well and make our leaders proud of whom we are as we learn to walk upright before the Lord. And surely let us not betray them or their trust in you.

THE RIGHT BETRAYER

"And while he yet spake, behold a multitude, and he that was called Judas, one of the twelve, went before them, and drew near unto Jesus to kiss him. But Jesus said unto him, Judas, betrayest thou the Son of man with a kiss?"

(Luke 22:47-48 KJV)

There is someone even assigned to you to betray you and we know that it will come from your inner cycle. Look around you and see who it is and guess what if you don't recognize who it is yet; it might be you....

It (your betrayer) has to be somebody that you trust and care about because they are the only ones who can get close enough to you and have the opportunity to betray you. It always comes, as a shocker because you never think a person that you trust would ever do anything as horrible and hurting as that. There is no explanation for a friend or family member who you truly walked with, trusted, and kept their secrets stab you in the back. Not only do they stab you but also they proceed to cut you like a razor on your jugular, then talk about you and lie on you. What is so amazing about all of this is you never expected it for to you there truly was no reason for the betrayal. For surely your enemy can, will, and shall betray you with a kiss just as Judas did Jesus.

However what I love about Jesus is He is a Redeemer not only from sin and death but also from defamation of character, as well as a healer of the betrayed. When people character assassinate you because of jealousy, envy or hatred and scandalize your name and try to destroy your integrity God will get up from the throne and come see about you. See God is not a respecter of persons for it doesn't matter to Him whether it is laity or a Pastor He will redeem you before the people and put you back in your rightful place in the Kingdom. What I have learned is that your betrayer becomes your elevator and if you can pass the test and not get angry, vengeful or bitter you can and will find yourself in the penthouse with God. Now understand that on your way to the penthouse make sure you receive Gods healing so you don't become someone else's betrayer and cause them the hurt and heartache that someone caused you. In this Christian walk I have learned we must all have a Judas but we don't all have to be a Judas. For remember as Christians we are to be like Jesus not like Judas...

A Right Heart: A Servant Heart

"Create in me a clean heart, O God; and renew a right spirit within me. Cast me not away from thy presence; and take not thy holy spirit from me. Restore unto me the joy of thy salvation; and uphold me with thy free spirit. Then will I teach

> *transgressors thy ways; and sinners shall be converted unto thee."*
>
> *(Psalms 51:10-13 KJV)*

The first thing that you must receive from God is a clean heart. You notice the word said create in me a clean heart for even if we are born with one, life's experiences of hurt, pain and people has tainted our hearts towards one another; and even towards God. See in order to do the work of ministry you must have a pure heart and correct motives or else you won't last long. Your heart must be bent toward God and the work of the Kingdom. You must put your needs and wants on the back burner and place Gods will for your life first. That means you must develop a servants heart for God. When you get at this level of ministry you realize that it is not about me, myself, or I but about doing the will of the Father that sent you. If you have a servant's heart you are called many unseeingly things by the people but you are a delight to God. For it is when you can serve others diligently and with the right attitude that God can trust you.

For the word of the Lord says if you are faithful over a few things God will make you ruler over much. All of this is a process a servants heart does not come overnight neither does a clean heart. A clean heart must come from God and it requires obedience and much repentance as we walk through this road called life. Now a servant's heart comes through many trials and tribulations as well as humility to the word of God and to the people of God. Only after God has created in you a clean heart, restored you, renewed a right spirit within you, can you receive the true joy of your salvation and become a willing servant for the Most High God. For truly "The sacrifices of God are a broken spirit: a broken and a contrite heart, O God, thou wilt not despise." (Psalms 51:17 KJV)

Christ had such a servant's heart toward His father that He was obedient unto death. Can you serve God under these conditions and still be faithful enough to trust Him with your life. You must have a servant's heart for God and nothing else.

Forgiving Heart

"So likewise shall my heavenly Father do also unto you, if ye from your hearts forgive not every one his brother their trespasses."

(Matthew 18:35 KJV)

I specifically separated this one out because many of us are stuck in a place called Lodi bar because of unforgiveness. We haven't forgiven the people that have offended or hurt us but most of all we haven't forgiven ourselves. So we remain stuck and can't move on because the enemy keeps reminding you of all of your failures, hurts and pains. Telling you in your mind they are not for you, watch her or him and trust no one anymore. See these are the tricks and schemes of the enemy to keep you in bondage and hold you back. I charge you to seek God, ask for forgiveness, forgive yourself, receive it in your mind and your spirit, and go forward with your life. Make up in your mind and heart that you are moving on and let no one or anything stop you from having a forgiving heart. I never said it would be easy but what I do know that it is attainable for I have done it. So now I can go forward into the call God has for my life without any guilt, or bitterness but with LOVE...

THE RIGHT CALL

"Then said the king to the servants, Bind him hand and foot, and take him away, and cast him into outer darkness; there shall be weeping and gnashing of teeth. For many are called, but few are chosen."

(Matthew 22:13-14 KJV)

What is called? To be *called* according to the dictionary means to order or undertake a particular activity or work; summon. Now when you look at this scripture it speaks in turns of many are called to salvation. This call goes out weekly at every church as well as daily through the Christian (believer of Christ) who share the Gospel with non-believers. Now the few that are chosen are the ones who answer the call, repent (turn away from their sins), and believe in Christ, they then are chosen to inherit the Kingdom of Heaven. In our lives we are called to many things but the right call that we must answer is the call to salvation through Jesus Christ. This call gives you the right to the Kingdom of God and all of its benefits, promises and statues. It is the only guarantee of eternal life according to the word of God. As Christians we must not scare people into salvation but speak life into them through the word of God and let Christ do the rest. For as the scripture said some plant and some water but God gives the increase. *"For while one saith,*

I am of Paul; and another, I am of Apollos; are ye not carnal? Who then is Paul, and who is Apollos, but ministers by whom ye believed, even as the Lord gave to every man? I have planted, Apollos watered; but God gave the increase. So then neither is he that planteth any thing, neither he that watereth; but God that giveth the increase." (1 Corinthians 3:4-7 KJV) It is just our job as Christians to plant or water for we cannot make and/or force anyone to accept the call to salvation.

FIVEFOLD MINISTRY

"And he gave some, apostles; and some, prophets; and some, evangelists; and some, pastors and teachers; For the perfecting of the saints, for the work of the ministry, for the edifying of the body of Christ: Till we all come in the unity of the faith, and of the knowledge of the Son of God, unto a perfect man, unto the measure of the stature of the fullness of Christ:"
(Ephesians 4:11-13 KJV)

Now this is also a call to be a gift to the Body of Christ (church) or ministry. These five gifts are for the building and the edification of the church. Each one having their own specific offices (job description) yet corporately needed to complete the church. Just to give a quick synopsis of the offices of the gifts to the church let's start with the Apostles who are called to establish the foundation of the church and sometimes even re-establish the church, they are the ones who have seen Christ and walked with Him (according to scripture). Now I know today that they say there are no more apostles but I beg to differ with that because at no point in the

Bible did you see where God said that He did away with any of the fivefold gifts. And as far as seeing and walking with Christ if Apostle Paul did it then why can't the apostles do it today. Christ had died and risen before Apostle Paul became an apostle. So Paul didn't actually see Jesus alive like Peter and John did but yet he is called one of the greatest apostles in the Bible and wrote most of the New Testament. This is not for argument sake just giving you a little food for thought and something to do a little more research on when you get a chance.

Next are the prophets now they are called to foretell and/or forth tell the future, they are known to be called the oracles of God (God's mouthpiece). Many do not believe in prophets as well anymore but once again I state the same argument I see nowhere in scripture where God said He did away with His prophets. Prophets are still very much needed in the church as seers, speakers, organizers and helpers to the Pastors. The evangelist is the person who has the special anointing on their life's to go out and win souls for Christ via the Gospel. This is the main reason why the churches exist, to go out and compel the lost to come in. The Pastors is the keeper of the flock and the shepherd over our souls. They are the ones who have Gods heart for His people? Last but not least we have the teacher, which is very much needed in the church because without knowledge and understanding we as a people will perish. For the word simply says; "My people perish from lack of knowledge."

The Right to Bind and Loose

"Verily I say unto you, Whatsoever ye shall bind on earth shall be bound in heaven: and whatsoever ye shall loose on earth shall be loosed in heaven. Again I say unto you, That if two of you shall agree on earth as touching any thing that they shall ask, it shall be done for them of my Father which is in heaven. For where two or three are gathered together in my name, there am I in the midst of them."

(Matthew 18:18-20 KJV)

When Jesus rose from the dead He rose with all power and He has given that power and authority to His disciples (Christ followers). One thing that is very important that we must learn is the power to bind and loose. What do I mean by that to bind means to tie, secure, restrain or bound? We have been given the right through Jesus Christ to tie up or bound the hands, schemes, plans, and tactics of the enemy. Some things that have entered into our churches, ministries, lives, marriages, and our homes are sent from the enemy to destroy us. But thanks be unto God who has given us the power to bind those things up and send them back to the very pit of hell where they have come from.

What we must understand is that we can only bind or loose through the power of His Name, His Blood, His Word and His Spirit. Now on the other hand we also have the power to loose some things in our life. To loose means to be free from confinement or imprisonment, to be released or uninhibited now when we look at it from this end we have the right to loose ourselves and our stuff from the hands of the enemy. For example a lot of times the enemy has our money bound up now there is two ways we loose our money. We asked God to loose it through the Holy Spirit and we loose it ourselves by following Gods word give and it shall be given to you pressed down shaken together and running over shall men give unto your bosom. See we must learn God's principles of binding and loosing it not just going to happen because you say it but there is a method to it. Not that I have the 411 on it because in Christ you are never full of His infinite knowledge but every day you are learning His ways, commands and statues. What I have learned in my walk with God is that the power of agreement can do more damage to the enemy then you could ever do by yourself. Yet the most important thing I must leave you with is this: *Bitterness binds but Love looses because without Love it is all-useless…*

THE RIGHT TO LIFT

"And, if I be lifted up from the earth, will draw all men unto me."

(John 12:32 KJV)

Although in the entire chapter I spoke about the Right Person and all the different attributes that Jesus possess. One thing we all must understand in ministry is that we have the right to lift Him up. What do I mean by that? That we as Christians should always be lifting up the name of Jesus, the life of Jesus, the victory we have through Jesus and the salvation we received through Jesus. See if we learn to lift Him up and not ourselves. Then we will realize that

He is the one who will draw all men to your church, enlarge your ministry, provide the scribe anointing so you can write prolific anointed books and develop you spiritually. It's through exalting Him and only Him can we be successful in all these things... *"And as Moses lifted up the serpent in the wilderness, even so must the Son of man be lifted up: That whosoever believeth in him should not perish, but have eternal life."* (John 3:14-15 KJV)

Chapter Three

The Right Medication (The Word)

THIS particular chapter of the book is derived from excerpts of writing as I dealt with the revelation of the word of God and compared it to life's experiences and situations that are going on in today's society. When you read these scriptures sometimes you may notice a shift in the anointing as God unveils His word to His people. For the word of God must be simple yet understandable and made relevant to today's times for us to be able to grasp it in the natural and spiritual realm. So as you read it know that each scripture can stand-alone or it may be a catalyst to the previous one. However you chose to see it doesn't matter as long as you receive the message that God has spoken and what I the writer am trying to convey to His people.

Now take heed that as you read this chapter it shall and will become medication to your soul. For when we start off with great expectation we can obtain that which we are looking for. May you find a healing, deliverance and an answer for the things that are present in your life? For I believe there is medication (a word) to soothe and solve all your problems in this chapter alone. For heaven and earth shall past away but the word of the Lord shall stand forever…

"In the beginning was the Word, and the Word was with God, and the Word was God." (John 1:1 KJV) As much as life has to offer us in this present world today nothing is greater or can be compared to the Word of God (The Bible). The word of God is awesome; it is a miracle working mystery sent from God. It has the power to do all things but fail. When Jesus was tempted by Satan in the wilderness it was the word that he used to defeat the devil. Jesus didn't try to use His divine power or His strength, which He could have. However Jesus chooses a different route He used **His Word.**

This was to show us that no matter what temptation or trials that you are facing, the word have the power and ability to deliver you from it all. See when we are tempted to do wrong or to bend the rules just a little bit we need to think back to what Jesus did. Many of us try to use our own strengths and knowledge to try to defeat our enemies but take heed to the Master Teacher and do what He did…***Use His Word!*** Then you will be able to stand through all of what life has to offer you both good and bad. Life is not always easy and sometimes it can be overwhelming but what I like about Gods word is it has the ability to shine light even in our darkest hours. So as you walk through this road called life never forget to get to know ***The WORD…***

Bread from Heaven

"But he answered and said, It is written, Man shall not live by bread alone, but by every word that proceedeth out of the mouth of God."

(Matthew 4:4 KJV)

Now in life there has to be something or someone that you use to base your destiny, plans and purpose on. Whatever you chose to use, it must be trustworthy and yet solid as a rock. Which means that the foundation must be built out of something that will not fail you, lie to you or disappoint you? The only thing that exists like that right now in this world is truly The Word. I mean the Bible (the infallible word of God) as well as the Living Word, which is Jesus. The word says man cannot live by bread alone. To me that mean you have to base your life on more than the physical of what you can see and what you can eat or take in. Naturally the bread of this world meaning the things of the flesh can never fulfill you. Why? Because man will always want more for the flesh is never satisfied.

However when you get a taste of the "Bread of Heaven" you no longer have a desire to eat from the earth. Your desire to consume heavenly things takes on a different meaning. See after eating from the "Bread of Life" you are no longer interested in doing the same old things but as you become new in Christ your interest change. You find yourself consuming the word of God more and prayer becomes a necessity instead of an option. You begin to find yourself praying things like Bread of Heaven feed me until I want no more. You now realize the word mixed with prayer has become medication to your soul. For as you continue to read, and study the scriptures it becomes like a ***permanent anesthetic/pain reliever*** (it numbs and kills the pain) those things that use to cause pain in your life have been healed by the revealing word of God. The word can also bring down the heat like an ***antipyretic, which reduces fever.*** You find yourself no longer being heated by anger but heated by the consuming fire, which is the Holy Spirit that has attached itself to the word and made it become active and alive. Now the word can also be compared to an ***antibiotic.*** See the word will kill and destroy all the bacteria that Satan has tried to poison your mind, body and spirit with. Though I could use many ways to describe the word of God and its effect on us I chose to use the classifications of medicines because all can easily understand it. For all of us has used at least one of these medications if not all at one time or another.

> *"Pleasant words are as an honeycomb, sweet to the soul, and health to the bones."*
>
> *(Proverbs 16:24 KJV)*

See Gods word is so complex and complete that it can even be considered pleasant words meaning it leaves a pleasing result in your heart and mind as you read it and it ministers to you. Then you find out that it is not only pleasant but it is sweet as a honeycomb to your soul. Now when we break this down in naturalistic terms the word has become appealing, appetizing, and tasty to your mind, intellect and your will and now you have developed an appetite for it. And as you begin to feed on the word or as we sometimes say eat the word it becomes health (a condition of well being) to our bones (flesh or body). So when we look at all the things that pleasant words can do for us as well as for our mind (soul) and body why would we speak anything differently. Yet we speak many times negatively or according to what we see instead of what the word says. So let us learn to speak pleasant words so that the Lord will be pleased in how we speak and shed light (give revelation) on those things in which you say and do.

LIGHTED WORD

"The entrance of thy words giveth light; it giveth understanding unto the simple."

(Psalms 119:130 KJV)

Now I found this scripture very interesting for we can take it literally or figuratively. Let's take our mind on a little trip as we watch the word enter into our mouth. Think about it as it enters it begins to shine a light on everything inside your mouth. The first thing that would happen is all the impurities; cavities and plaque would show up. Then when you look closer you would begin to see decay and maybe broken or chipped teeth. Later as you kept on looking you would notice that there are some false teeth, dentures or implants and if you begin to investigate a little further you would notice gingivitis or maybe even an abscess. Now that we have had a vivid look into the mouth via the lighted word now we can get a clear understanding of how the word shines light on all our faults, issues and bad habits. Exposing all things that were hidden and in the dark, making it plain and simple what the problems are, and how to deal with them. The purpose of the light is for you to see better, so you can do better.

We can only do better if we understand better, which leads me to our next scripture.

> *"That we henceforth be no more children, tossed to and fro, and carried about with every wind of doctrine, by the sleight of men, and cunning craftiness, whereby they lie in wait to deceive; But speaking the truth in love, may grow up into him in all things, which is the head, even Christ: From whom the whole body fitly joined together and compacted by that which every joint supplieth, according to the effectual working in the measure of every part, maketh increase of the body unto the edifying of itself in love."*
>
> *(Ephesians 4:14-16 KJV)*

This scripture is very critical because in the midst of all that you will go through you must be steadfast and unmovable always abounding in the work of the Lord and knowing that your labor is never in vain. See you got to know, that you know, that you know that Christ is all and there is no failure in him. When you are convinced of this no devil in hell can deceive you no matter how crafty it may seem or cunning he may be. For always remember God will never have you ignorant of your enemies and will always make a way of escape. When you are connected to the Lord many things are revealed or unveiled to us who believe and all things become new. If your connections are with the true and living God you cannot be tossed to and fro regardless of situations or circumstances. Come what may you are solidified in Christ speaking the truth in love, growing up into Him in all things, and jointly fitting and edifying the body of Christ through love. We must remember that deception has no place in God's house but love will always reside in God's house.

> *"Be not deceived; God is not mocked: for whatsoever a man soweth, that shall he also reap. For he that soweth to his flesh shall of the flesh reap corruption; but he that soweth to the Spirit shall of the Spirit reap life everlasting."*
>
> *(Galatians 6:7-8 KJV)*

For many years of my life I have heard this saying "You reap what you sow" and I literally thought it was a cliché. Then as I begin to learn the Bible I realized that it wasn't a cliché. It was a true fact and it was written in the Bible. Now we must go back to our teachings and understand that the Bible is the infallible word of God. That means everything written in it is true, holy, and righteous. Just as God is truth, holiness and righteousness so now when you think about that statement and/or scripture it should raise some questions in your mind. And the questions should be… **During my lifetime and even right now what have I sown and what shall I reap?**

Now according to scripture God is not deceived. Meaning you can fool people but at no time in life can you ever fool God. He knows exactly what you have sown and knows exactly what you will reap. Now if the truth were told all of us are reaping at least one thing that we know we are not deserving of; and that is eternal life. Now the next question is where will you spend it? Now that one is entirely up to you. My suggestion to you is that if you have not already sown your life into Christ hands then now would be a good time.

For those who are not sure how to do it let me help you. Here are the scriptures that you need to read and just follow Gods instructions (Rom 10:8-10 KJV) *"But what saith it? The word is nigh thee, even in thy mouth, and in thy heart: that is, the word of faith, which we preach; That if thou shalt confess with thy mouth the Lord Jesus, and shalt believe in thine heart that God hath raised him from the dead, thou shalt be saved. For with the heart man believeth unto righteousness; and with the mouth confession is made unto salvation."*

Thank God for salvation through Jesus Christ. For in the middle of all these economic uncertainties, wars and rumors of wars we need to know that there is someone we can count on besides man. When we look around at the world's situations and circumstance it looks pretty dim right now. For at no time in life are we to lean on man and man alone. We must trust completely in God even when it looks dark for He is the Light. Trust not in the flesh (the things of this world) for flesh only reaps flesh but rely on the spirit, which is God. He promises that you will reap the harvest of blessing not only here and now…but throughout eternity…and that is one of Gods greatest gifts to man.

CORRECTIVE WORD

No servant can serve two masters: for either he will hate the one, and love the other; or else he will hold to the one, and despise the other. Ye cannot serve God and mammon. And the Pharisees also, who were covetous, heard all these things: and they derided him. And he said unto them, Ye are they which justify yourselves before men; but God knoweth your hearts: for that which is highly esteemed among men is abomination in the sight of God."

(Luke 16:13-16 KJV)

Many times we read the Bible and we take some of the scriptures for granted never fully understanding what God is trying to convey to His people. . In whom do you trust? If your trust has been in man or money right about now you are in a lot of trouble; for man is financially unstable and money has lost its value. However what I have learned from all of this is that if you trust in God and serve Him you can never go wrong. God didn't say you would never have financial problems or have your personal trials and tribulations for truly these things are just a test of your faith. But what He did say is that if you serve Him then you cannot serve man and/or money.

I used this scripture for the simple fact you can only serve one master and that is God. If you try and serve anything or anyone else you are truly out of the will of God. It is never Gods intentions for you to serve anyone but Him in fact the word say seek the Kingdom of God first and all else will be added to you. So we don't have to seek money, man, things or success but if we seek God and the things of God first; God will guide and direct our paths. *Neither money nor man can give you any guarantees in life but truly our Great God is satisfaction and guaranteed to do everything He said and promised.* So, make sure as you journey through life you serve the right master and that is the One and Only, True and Living God. For certainly when you serve Him, He'll give favor, finances and deem you faithful…

> "*It is the spirit that quickeneth; the flesh profiteth nothing: the words that I speak unto you, they are spirit, and they are life.*" John 6:63 KJV

In this present world that we are living in right now there is not a whole lot of things to be happy or excited about. Everywhere we look we see misfortunes, murders or some type of mess going on. This is the time in life that we need to look for positive influences, reinforcements, and something or someone good we can depend on that won't change or fail. Well there is only one truly good person who doesn't change and His word never fails. So let me direct everyone to Jesus and the Bible, which is His word.

However there is a specific word that comes to mind *"It is the spirit that quickeneth; the flesh profiteth nothing:* **the words that I speak unto you, they are spirit, and they are life.***"* Let's look at this scripture carefully and evaluate what we speak and ourselves. Are we speaking life through the spirit or death through our flesh? What words are you finding in your vocabulary are they words that discourage your friends and family or do your words encourage them and bring life and hope to them? Can they depend on you to speak the truth through faith according to the word of God?

See your words can kill or build, can cut or heal, can destroy or develop a person, a situation or a problem. Evaluate yourself, have you been building or killing the people around you. Either way it is never too late for change. We as Christians or even non-believers never want to speak death into anyone's life or current situations. We must let them know that in every circumstance there is always hope, for we are never left hopeless with Jesus Christ. For we serve a God who gives us specific instructions on the power of the tongue. He simply said these words in Proverbs 18:21 KJV *"Death and life are in the power of the tongue: and they that love it shall eat the fruit thereof."*

So use the power of your tongue for good and speak life, love and faith into everything and watch how God turn your bad into good. For truly when you're speaking changes, your mind changes (becomes renewed) and your perception change. Then and only then can we speak and see as Christ does…

Spoken Word

"But the LORD said unto me, Say not, I am a child: for thou shalt go to all that I shall send thee, and whatsoever I command thee thou shalt speak. Be not afraid of their faces: for I am with thee to deliver thee, saith the LORD."

(Jeremiah 1:7-8 KJV)

No matter what age you are in the natural or in the spirit when God releases you to go or speak for Him we cannot worry about what people think or what their faces look like. Their faces are just an indication of where they are at naturally or spiritually. Sometimes it can be an eye opener to what they think or believe. We must at no time during our walk with God put people's opinions and desires over God's instructions. Now understand me clearly I am not saying at no time are you to be disobedient to your leaders or Pastors nor out of order. If God has truly given you the word to speak or work to do He will make a way even if He has to move you. Many times we are intimidated by people because of their titles or positions and so we believe that they know more or hear better from God than we do. Only to find out that although you may be a child in the Gospel God still can use you to give an adult (mature saint) a word. However it is up to them whether they want to receive it. This is a Selah moment (a moment to pause and think, and reflect on what was just said).

"This book of the law shall not depart out of thy mouth; but thou shalt meditate therein day and night, that thou mayest

observe to do according to all that is written therein: for then thou shalt make thy way prosperous, and then thou shalt have good success."

(Joshua 1:8 KJV)

Now as we close this chapter there is no better way to end it then with this scripture. No matter what the situation or circumstances never let this Bible depart from you. It is your means of survival and your means of healing and deliverance. It is the word of God that will set the captive free from all of the world's mess. You are to meditate on it day and night. Simply meaning all the time: so that you may become a doer of the word and not a hearer only. See when you become a doer of the word you find yourself becoming prosperous and very successful. Now surely that alone should be medication for your soul.

Chapter Four

THE RIGHT TIME

You have the right to be in Gods timing!

As we go through life everyone has the right to be in God's timing as a matter of fact the world works according to what God allows. Moment by moment, hour by hour, day by day, month by month, and year by year is all going according to Gods timing and divine purpose. When we think of the word time it could have many meaning but for the sake of understanding this chapter I will use the following definitions. Time meaning a suitable or opportune moment or season, an appointed or fated moment and last but not least an interval esp. a span of years, marked by similar events, conditions, or phenomena; an era.

There is at no time any place in this world, atmosphere or hemi-sphere that God does not know what is happening whether it be good or bad and at no time does any situation or circumstance surprise God or catch Him off guard. We must understand that God is Alpha and Omega the beginning and the end. Nothing was started without Him and all things are completed through Him. He is the first and the last for He is simply God and there is no other. He is the creator of all things and without Him nothing was made. The Lord is so awesome that He didn't use his hands to create He just spoke the word and time, seasons, purpose and everything else came into existence. Now that's why we call Him sovereign and the Great I Am for who else can create a world with words and everything you spoke remains constant and obedient without change.

> *"To every thing there is a season, and a time to every purpose under the heaven: A time to be born, and a time to die; a time to plant, and a time to pluck up that which is planted; A time to kill, and a time to heal; a time to break down, and a time to build up;" A time to weep, and a time to laugh; a time to mourn, and a time to dance; A time to cast away stones, and a time to gather stones together; a time to embrace, and a time to refrain from embracing; A time to get, and a time to lose; a time to keep, and a time to cast away; A time to rend, and a time to sew; a time to keep silence, and a time to speak; A time to love, and a time to hate; a time of war, and a time of peace. What profit hath he that worketh in that wherein he laboureth?"*
>
> *(Ecclesiastes 3:1-9 KJV)*

As the verse says to everything there is a season and a time for every purpose under heaven. A *season* is a recurrent period characterized by certain occurrences, occupations, festivities, or crops;

a suitable, natural or convenient time or a period of time; and the word *purpose* means the object toward which one strives or for which something exists; an aim or goal; a result or an effect that is intended or desired; an intention. Notice the sequence in which God said it. The season came first because it is characterized by a specific amount of time and according to events, situations or occurrences where as time has no limits and it never stops it keeps on going whether you are sleep or awake, dead or alive. Now purpose on the other hand is specific again this time according to the person, place, or thing not everyone or every object has the same purpose or value. Nevertheless let's move on to the purpose of your time and season here on earth.

At this season in your life you ought to be striving to become the light in a dark world or to become the salt of the earth truly bringing God's flavor to everything we do or say. This is the time to get into Gods presence and develop a true relationship with Him. To learn who God is for yourself not according to what other people say or what you may feel or think. Let it be a fact that you have gotten to know and have established an intimate relationship with the Savior (Jesus Christ).

SALVATION TIME

Prior to this reading if you did not know Christ in the pardon of your sins then let us take time to give you the opportunity now. For simply in Romans 10:8-9 says *"But what saith it? The word is nigh thee, even in thy mouth, and in thy heart: that is, the word of faith, which we preach; That if thou shalt confess with thy mouth the*

Lord Jesus, and shalt believe in thine heart that God hath raised him from the dead, thou shalt be saved. For with the heart man believeth unto righteousness; and with the mouth confession is made unto salvation." Now that you have received salvation there are some other times that we can look forward to and yet some times we must be careful of. One thing we can look forward to is prayer time with the Lord. However what we must watch out for is the enemy during our lifetime or shall I say at all times.

WATCH AND PRAY

"Take ye heed, watch and pray: for ye know not when the time is. For the Son of man is as a man taking a far journey, who left his house, and gave authority to his servants, and to every man his work, and commanded the porter to watch."

(Mark 13:33-34 KJV)

There comes a time in a Christian's life where they mature in the things of the Lord and begin to develop what I call the skills of warfare. The first two most important skills are developing a prayer life so that you can hear clearly from God and second is becoming a watchman for Christ's Kingdom. When you develop these two you are not easily deceived by people or the devil (Satan). Prayer is your communication line with God. Prayer is where you get your instructions, guidance, blessings and promises from God. It is also the place where you get cleansed, chastised, refined, and equipped for battle. Reaching our destiny in our spiritual life and our natural life relies a lot on our prayer life. Prayer can keep you one-step ahead of your enemies and it also gives you power (authority) over the enemy, which is Satan. Tapping into God's presence (through prayer) and using the Holy Spirit as your revealer makes your spiritual walk a heck of a lot easier for although we don't have all the answer we can truly avoid some unnecessary trials and tribulations. Now that we have established what prayer can do for you let's look at what a watchmen can do and how important it is in this season to have a watchmen's spirit.

What exactly is a watchman it is literally just what it says someone who watches in the natural as well as in the spirit realm. A watchman is what I call or shall I say our protection in the spirit. He has the ability to see and give you a warning, or an opportunity to avoid things in the natural and/or in the spirit. However as watchmen you can't always reveal what you see; you must use your spiritual discernment (insight). Before you speak to anyone about anything make sure you understand what you see before you release it. For it may not be time yet…

It is not time yet

"Then Jesus said unto them, My time is not yet come: but your time is alway ready. The world cannot hate you; but me it hateth, because I testify of it, that the works thereof are evil. Go ye up unto this feast: I go not up yet unto this feast: for my time is not yet full come."

(John 7:6-8 KJV)

There is a time to and a season for everyone to learn and be patient. We must learn that we have to move on God's timing and not ours. You must be careful because the devil will make you believe one of two things; it is time (to go forth in your purpose and destiny) when it is not or either it is not time, when it is. You have to be like Jesus and not move before your time even when everyone around you seems to be going forth in purpose. Let's be honest before you move into the promises and blessings God has for us; there are some test we must go through and pass. If the truth were told by the seasoned saints (Christians) you have to walk through some stuff. Things like persecution from the church and your fellow Christians, unbelief and wavering faith, hatred from the unbelievers, betrayal and defamation of your character. These trials and tribulations are not options but necessary experiences to get you to where God has ordained for you to go. Many times as you are suffering and being tried by the fire (tested by trials) it appears that everyone else seems to be feasting on the good things of life. Even if everyone else is feasting and you are suffering know God has not forgotten you and while you are waiting for Him to redeem you out of these horrible tests and trials be faithful, steadfast, and unmovable knowing that your labor with God is never in vain.

In the Midst of Your Waiting Whatever He Says Do.

"Jesus saith unto her, Woman, what have I to do with thee? mine hour is not yet come. His mother saith unto the servants, Whatsoever he saith unto you, do it."

(John 2:4-5 KJV)

Now earlier in this chapter we learned not to move before your time and be patient in the midst of your tests, trials, and tribulations. But there was one thing that I forgot to mention in all of your waiting whatever God says do. It (God's instructions) may not always make sense and you may not even understand them but if you know for sure that God said it then do it. That's what we call *walking by faith and not by sight*. See faith makes us do what we can't see or comprehend but yet we believe. We believe in Jesus enough to be obedient to the words He speaks whether it comes from the prophet, a pastor, a Christian, or a revelation from the Bible. When we look back at some of the greatest people in the Bible they became great because of their faith walk with God. They did what God said even when everything and everyone seem to be against it. For example Noah built an Ark for a flood and had never even seen rain, Abraham and Sarah believed God for a son even in their old age, and let's not forget in the New Testament how many times someone's faith made them whole. All of this was an example of how you can start out one way and your faith in God and obedience to His word and His ways can create a miracle in your life. Although we never like waiting on God or steeping out on faith what we have learned is that this appears to be Gods process or one of His ways of blessing His people. So remember in the midst of waiting whatever God says do and you will walk right into your appointed time and season.

The Appointed Time /Vision Time

"I will stand upon my watch, and set me upon the tower, and will watch to see what he will say unto me, and what I shall

answer when I am reproved. And the LORD answered me, and said, Write the vision, and make it plain upon tables, that he may run that readeth it. For the vision is yet for an appointed time, but at the end it shall speak, and not lie: though it tarry, wait for it; because it will surely come, it will not tarry.'

(Habakkuk 2:1-3 KJV)

There is an appointed time and season for us all. Now getting to it takes a lot of faith, obedience, testing, and prayer. The funny thing about your appointed time (for purpose, destiny and/or a miracle) is it seems like it takes forever for God to do what He promised. Then all of a sudden you look up and you are there. Now let us backtrack a minute first God will give you a word, then He will give you a promise, next He gives you a test, and last but not least He will bring it (whatever He promised you) to pass. Once you get that word or promise from God it always seem that the opposite starts to happen in your life. For example God promises you that you will become a millionaire then all of a sudden you are broke. Your finances seem to become attacked. First you lose your job, and then you lose your car, then your house and before you know it everything is lost and all you have are your faith and a promise from God. In the midst of all this you have watched to see how God is going to step in but there still seems to be no God. Then all out of nowhere here comes God and to your avail He did it on a simple idea that He gave you. He told you to write a book and so you write the vision and make it plain. Then your writing turns into editor and the book turns into a miracle and blesses you beyond measures and you find just that quick your appointed time and vision has come to pass. For God just opened a door for you that no man could shut but know that there are many adversaries. For your faith will be challenged by the adversary over and all over again but thank God for the Comforter (Holy Spirit) that is our helper through all things.

COMFORTER

"And I will pray the Father, and he shall give you another Comforter, that he may abide with you for ever; Even the Spirit of truth; whom the world cannot receive, because it seeth him not, neither knoweth him: but ye know him; for he dwelleth with you, and shall be in you."

(John 14:16-17KJV)

Now let's understand what or shall I say who the Comforter is. The Comforter is the third person of the Trinity or Godhead. The Godhead consists of the Father, the Son, and the Holy Spirit. Three separate persons yet all one God. That in itself is a mystery by God. The Holy Spirit is sent by God to the believer to comfort, teach, guide, and help you. This Holy Spirit is not someone you can see but it is the spirit of God that will live or shall I say dwell inside you. The Holy Spirit is given to the believer when you receive salvation. Once you are saved/rescued from the enemy, which is Satan you need someone to help you live this Christian life. The Holy Spirit does just that. He makes it possible to go through all of the suffering, hurt and pain. He also makes it possible for you to understand the Bible and all of Gods ways. He gives you great revelation on how and why Jesus died for us and teaches us the true doctrine of the Godhead. You may wonder why I didn't say this first but I wanted you to read about all the different times and seasons in your life. Then I wanted to remind you that there is a helper and a comforter that Jesus promised to send us when He ascended back to the Father. He is our "Paracletos" for the Holy Spirit is the one who walks alongside you and comforts you through all of life's situations and circumstances whether good, bad, or indifferent. More important than that He is the one that will quicken your mortal body to be rapture up when Jesus returns. Now that alone is a reason to thank God for sending His Holy Spirit that whom we call the Comforter. For the Comforter will help you, guide you, teach you, and comfort you while you are living on earth and usher you into eternity at the appointed time when you die.

Eternity Time

> *"Let not your heart be troubled: ye believe in God, believe also in me. In my Father's house are many mansions: if it were not so, I would have told you. I go to prepare a place for you. And if I go and prepare a place for you, I will come again, and receive you unto myself; that where I am, there ye may be also. And whither I go ye know, and the way ye know."*
>
> *(John 14:1-4 KJV)*

In all that we go through in life God has made preparations for each and every situation. In His love for us not only did He die so we could have an abundant life while on earth but in His wisdom He remembers our eternal destination. Life is just a short span of years maybe one year or maybe even a hundred compared to eternity. What makes God so mystical and yet the Great I Am is He prepared eternity for us and told us what we can look forward to. That there is two choices heaven or hell and He explains them both. Now the choice is purely up to you where you will spend eternity. I pray after reading this book that you choose heaven as your destination and certainly not hell. Why would you not want to spend eternity with the true and living God? Where there will be no more worries, pain and suffering but a place where peace and love will abide forever. A place that Jesus personally said He has prepared for you. Where the streets are paved with gold and mansions are your home without struggle and a mortgage to worry about. Not that we have earned it because of anything we have done but only through Christ death and our choice to choose salvation and sanctification. We as Christians must realize that life down here is only a dress rehearsal for our eternal destination. For what you do down here on earth will determine where you go for eternity. So make the right decisions while living on earth and choose Jesus for Eternity… *"I said in mine heart, God shall judge the righteous and the wicked: for there is a time there for every purpose and for every work." (Ecclesiastes 3:17 KJV)*

AT NO TIME DO WE EVER ENTERTAIN THE DEVIL!

Chapter Five

The Right Dose
(Faith and the Anointing)

"For I say, through the grace given unto me, to every man that is among you, not to think of himself more highly than he ought to think; but to think soberly, according as God hath dealt to every man the measure of faith."

(Romans 12:3 KJV)

What is Faith?

ALL of Gods people have the right to a dose of the anointing and faith, now how much you acquire will be solely up to you. For Gods faith, power, and anointing is limitless and the more you hunger and thirst after righteousness the more you will be fed. It is never Gods intention for us to go hungry or thirsty for anything. God is Jehovah Jireh, which means He is our provider and He shall and will supply all of our needs. As Christians we must develop our faith enough to believe that even in times of a drought or a struggle God will provide. Now what is faith and how do we get it? *"Now faith is the substance of things hoped for, the evidence of things not seen." (Hebrews 11:1 KJV)*

Faith is believing God for something you can't see, hear, or maybe not even understand. You truly have no way humanly possible of seeing it. It must be seen through the eyes of faith. Meaning neither the carnal mind nor the five senses can comprehend it (faith). Faith is just stepping out on God's word and guidance even when it doesn't make sense to our natural mind. Faith can get you things from God that hard work could never get you. For through faith we can move mountains and obtain blessings and promises that only can be given to you by God. God is the only one who has the power and the ability to bypass the natural recommendations and/or requirements. See faith is the blessed hope and the sure knowledge that God is able to do everything but fail and nothing is impossible for Him.

To understand faith you must get to know God for Jesus was the epitome of faith. Jesus is our true and living example of faith. He trusted and believed in all Gods promises, blessings, commands, and statues. He never wavered in anything that the Father said to Him; for He trusted wholly and completely in everything the Father said. Why did He trust the Father simply put in the words of Jesus "For I and the Father are one, if you have seen me then you have seen the Father." See faith and the Trinity (The Father, The Son, and The Holy Spirit) are truly the mysteries of the Bible. You can't see them with your natural eyes but surely you know that they exist.

How do we Get Faith?

How do we get faith? "So then faith cometh by hearing, and hearing by the word of God." (Romans 10:17 KJV) Now we just learned what faith is and now here in this scripture God has given us an answer to our question. So faith comes by hearing now let us look at the word hearing. Hearings definition is *the sense by which sound is perceived; the capacity to hear.* Now let us look at the word hear which is the verb. Hear means *to perceive sound by the ear* but let's go a little further into the definition it also means *to listen to attentively, to learn by hearing; be told by others, to receive news or information; learn.* These extensive definitions take you to another place and give you a lot more detail on how to receive faith. It goes much further than just hearing the word of God through the audible sound.

Not only must you hear it through your natural ear but also you must listen attentively and learn. See faith comes by learning Gods word (The Bible), being watchful, and paying attention to detail. As we read Romans 10:17 and did a little research and expounding we found out that the word of God is not always as simple as it may sound. However to get full understanding of God's word we must sometimes pray, read other scriptures, and look up some vocabulary words in the dictionary. We must go to all lengths to get a good revelation (supernatural or divine meaning) of the word of God. The more we know and understand the more our faith increases.

The more your faith increases the more you began to exercise Gods principles in your life. This is when you become a doer of the word not just a hearer. Now remember we just learned that a hearer was a person who paid close attention to God's word and learned it. Now you have moved on to the next level for you are now performing that which you have just learned. So you have moved from faith to faith. "So, as much as in me is, I am ready to preach the gospel to you that are at Rome also. For I am not ashamed of the gospel of Christ: for it is the power of God unto salvation to everyone that believeth; to the Jew first, and also to the Greek. For therein is the righteousness of God revealed from faith to faith: as it is written, The just shall live by faith." (Romans 1:15-17 KJV)

Levels of Faith

There are many levels of faith that are spoken about in the Bible. There is a measure of faith, which is given to everyone that believes. There is mountain-moving faith that is also known as mustard seed faith. Then there is an anointing of faith that gives you the power to lay hands on the sick and they will recover. This faith is spoken about in Mark 16:15-18 KJV "And he said unto them, Go ye into all the world, and preach the gospel to every creature. He that believeth and is baptized shall be saved; but he that believeth not shall be damned. And these signs shall follow them that believe; In my name shall they cast out devils; they shall speak with new tongues; They shall take up serpents; and if they drink any deadly thing, it shall not hurt them; they shall lay hands on the sick, and they shall recover."

This is the kind of faith that destroys yokes. To the saint or the believer it is known as yoke breaking faith because it can destroy or simply annihilate anything, any demon, or any stronghold. *"And it shall come to pass in that day, that his burden shall be taken away from off thy shoulder, and his yoke from off thy neck, and the yoke shall be destroyed because of the anointing." (Isaiah 10:27 KJV)* See when you mix faith with the anointing it creates miracles, signs, and wonders. The anointing is simply Gods spirit within you and upon you that will cause the supernatural to interject into a situation and cause an unexplainable change or charge.

The Anointing
"But the anointing which ye have received of him abideth in you, and ye need not that any man teach you: but as the same anointing teacheth you of all things, and is truth, and is no lie, and even as it hath taught you, ye shall abide in him."
(1 John 2:27 KJV)

No man can teach you or give you God's anointing it must come from God himself. Now the anointing represents many things for example it represents God's presence, God's spirit (Holy Spirit), God's power, and God's empowerment. As believers we rely on the anointing from God to do the work that He has called us to do. Many can preach, sing, praise, and worship in the ministry but it is the anointing that makes the difference between being effective or ineffective in your calling. See when the anointing (God's presence and Spirit) is ushered into the room things begin to change. For everything is subject to the true and living God. Why? Because when He spoke all things came into existence for He is the creator of everything. Whatever is not like God will be exposed and the Spirit of truth will reveal and teach you all things. It is God's spirit that teaches us and guides us to our calling and gives us true understanding of who we are.

It is the anointing from God that empowers the believer with the ability to use the gifts that God has bestowed upon them. Many believers have the gifts (whether they are governmental or congregational) but they are not empowered to demonstrate them. See God must anoint you for divine service. *"And thou shalt put them upon Aaron thy brother and his sons with him; and shalt anoint them, and consecrate them, and sanctify them, that they may minister unto me in the priest's office." (Exodus 28:41 KJV)*

You must not only be called but you must be anointed and appointed and set aside for the master's use. Now this is a process it is not something that comes over night. Yes the anointing can rest upon you for a temporary assignment as in Old Testament days but with the new covenant the anointing abides in the believers. The anointing that abides in you helps you grasp and execute your basic ministerial duties. The anointing imparts the divine powers needed for service to the Lord and it also concurrently activates the hidden powers and talents of the minister. The anointing makes ministry easy and gives you the ability to deliver the word with power and authority. For your dependency is on God and not yourself. God's presence,

God's spirit, and God's power which is the anointing gives you the capability and potency to deliver, heal, and liberate God's people. Now I have talked about faith and the anointing as two separate entities but now let's mix the two.

FAITH AND THE ANOINTING

"And it came to pass, when they were gone over, that Elijah said unto Elisha, Ask what I shall do for thee, before I be taken away from thee. And Elisha said, I pray thee, let a double portion of thy spirit be upon me. And he said, Thou hast asked a hard thing: nevertheless, if thou see me when I am taken from thee, it shall be so unto thee; but if not, it shall not be so."

(2 Kings 2:9-10 KJV)

Faith and the anointing are two invisible supernatural concepts but yet when you mix them together they manifest a natural result. I used this scripture because it represented all that could be manifested from a mixture of faith and the anointing. Elijah and Elisha both had to have faith in God. For Elijah knew that he would be taken away yet he never feared, complained or questioned God. He had what I would call radical faith because in the midst of him being taken away he was concerned about his successors needs. He didn't ask God for anything for himself as many of us do but he asked Elisha before I am taken away what shall I (Elijah) do for you (Elisha). Wow is that not a true servants heart yet a great leader's quality. Elijah knew through faith that it was not about Him but it was about continuing the work of the

Lord. So He proposed a very important question to Elisha. Surely this had to be the anointing of God that would answer Elijah like this. Not that Elisha wanted a car, a house, a great position but He said something profound.

He did not become coveted but Elisha recognized that his need goes beyond what he can see. Elisha did not ask for anything physical from Elijah, as many of the saints today would have done. His faith recognized that what Elijah had spiritually was much greater than anything naturally that he could ask for. So he requests that he receive a double portion of Elijah spirit (which was God's anointing) to be upon him. Now not only did it take faith to say that but also it took a greater faith to believe it. Nevertheless Elisha received it by faith for he stood steadfast and stayed the course to receive the double portion of the anointing that was on Elijah's life.

See it is the nevertheless blessings that will create a miracle in your life just as it did for Elisha and Elijah. Elijah never doubted or discouraged Elisha but He challenged him. In reality Elijah said to Elisha truly nothing is impossible for God if you just believe. So what we have just witnessed here is faith plus the anointing even in Old Testament times caused signs and wonders to follow them. For Elisha was able to do twice as many miracles as Elijah had done.

So I say to you the readers as Elijah said to Elisha: "Though you have asked a hard thing if you see Him, believe in Him, and remember the just shall live by faith." See the anointing will be the key ingredient to work your faith and receive a miracle."

> *"By faith Enoch was translated that he should not see death; and was not found, because God had translated him: for before his translation he had this testimony, that he pleased God. But without faith it is impossible to please him: for he that cometh to God must believe that he is, and that he is a rewarder of them that diligently seek him."*
>
> *(Hebrews 11:5-6 KJV)*

Now as I close this chapter and move on I pray that you have learned that without faith it is impossible to please God and without God's anointing you cannot destroy yokes. However even with faith and the anointing you still must take the right route to get to your destiny and that is through the Cross.

Chapter Six

The Right Route

You have the right to take Gods route through the Cross-to your purpose, plan, and destiny…

"Likewise also the chief priests mocking him, with the scribes and elders, said, He saved others; himself he cannot save. If he be the King of Israel, let him now come down from the cross, and we will believe him."

(Matthew 27:41-42 KJV)

IN order for you to be effective and authentic you must come through the right route as Jesus did through the line of David. See there are two main routes according to scripture one is your lineage (bloodline) and the other is the Cross. The right route, which comes through the Cross, includes your salvation and all that is included in the Bible from start to finish. Naturally there is a process for all things and God is the director of the process. Now when we talk about the right routes we must start at the Cross-where Jesus suffered and die. The Cross-is the place that represents or shall I say symbolizes the Christian faith. For it is there that all our sins were nailed to the Cross right along with our Savior. To lots of people back in Jesus days the cross was a place of public disgrace, humiliation, and torture for the criminals. We all know that Jesus was neither but it was the route that He must take to get to His destiny. The death on the cross was just the fulfillment of Gods plan for redemption of mankind. The road to the cross was not easy neither was it delightful or joyous but it was harsh and cruel but yet absolutely necessary. See if Jesus had come down from the Cross-we would still be lost.

When we look back at the Book of the prophet Isaiah; we can learn a lot about the coming Messiah and His route to the Cross.

WOUNDED AND REJECTED

"He is despised and rejected of men; a man of sorrows, and acquainted with grief: and we hid as it were our faces from him; he was despised, and we esteemed him not. Surely he hath borne our griefs, and carried our sorrows: yet we did esteem him stricken, smitten of God, and afflicted. But he was wounded for our transgressions, he was bruised for our iniquities: the chastisement of our peace was upon him; and with his stripes we are healed."

(Isaiah 53:3-5 KJV)

Why must Jesus be rejected? For many of us know that once God speaks a word into the atmosphere it must come to pass. We also know that the word must be tried by the devil and we must be tested in our faith. When we look at the prophets of old they prophesied Jesus plan, purpose, and destiny. Isaiah talked about His rejection, His wounds, His afflictions, and His despising. His rejection was due to the fact He wasn't what they expected and His plan was not what they had in mind. They wanted someone to come and save them from the Roman government. However Jesus came to save them from the serpent. No one could understand this method because just as the Bible says His ways are not like our ways. See they were looking for a temporary solution to one problem and Jesus had come with a permanent solution to all problems. It was no secret to God that Jesus would be rejected because it was all in God's plan. For if the serpent/ devil would have understood the plan He would be the sovereign one instead of God.

So your peers must reject you as well when it comes to Gods plan in your life. Just as the Sadducees, the Pharisees, and the Jews rejected Jesus you as a believer will and shall walk in a similar situation. Many of us have already been tested and tried by our peers and found guilty of being in God's will. See Gods will for your life will cause people to reject you for many reasons mainly for jealousy, envy, or covetousness. See you are only rejected (unwanted) and despised (hated) because of what's in you or what you stand for. In the case of the Christian who is living right and walking into their calling they are persecuted for righteousness sake. What do I mean by this? When you get saved and begin to live a life that is pleasing to God many people begin to turn on you (reject or despise). Why? Because they either don't want you to change, they don't like the change, or because it is forcing them to look at themselves and make a change.

What I can say to all of the believers is change is a hard thing to do and accept. That's why as you begin to change from faith to faith and glory-to-glory you experience bruising and wounding from the world and the church. The believers as well as the non-believers begin to prejudge you, lie on you, and mistreat you because of your anointing and the call that is on your life. The sad part is the believers are the worst persecutors because they have become traditional and stuck in certain doctrines just as the Pharisee and Sadducees had become. The same goes on today; very few leaders are looking at the anointing or healing power of the believer. They are looking at their credentials and where they came from or whom do they sit under. If it does not add up to what they expect they reject, despise, bruise, or wound you. However if they read the Bible Jesus didn't add up to the expectations of the people either but it didn't mean He wasn't the Messiah. What ever happen to the bible sayings "try the spirit by the spirit"? *"Beloved, believe not every spirit, but try the spirits whether they are of God: because many false prophets are gone out into the world." (1 John 4:1 KJV)* What happen to spiritual discernment and prayer? These things have become secondary to tradition and doctrine. For many of us Christians miss our blessings by this behavior (tradition) and are blinded by the plan, schemes, and tactics of Satan. Yes I know we as leaders have to follow some rules and doctrines but it should never outweigh God's will. Nevertheless thank God for Jesus who bared all our sins, infirmities, and iniquities on the

Cross-at Calvary? Christ was crucified for us and now we must be crucified for Him.

CRUCIFIED WITH HIM

"And when they were come to the place, which is called Calvary, there they crucified him, and the malefactors, one on the right hand, and the other on the left. Then said Jesus, Father, forgive them; for they know not what they do. And they parted his raiment, and cast lots."

(Luke 23:33-34 KJV)

He wasn't just killed but He was crucified. Now what's the difference between the two? When you're killed it could be by accident, mistaken identity or many other means and sometimes even done on purpose. However when you are crucified you are killed and tortured by being nailed to death. To crucify means to put to death by nailing or binding to a cross; to mortify or subdue the flesh or to treat cruelly. Now Jesus went through them all. He was crucified in the flesh first. For the scripture simply says he was bruised, wounded, despised and rejected, smitten and they esteemed Him not.

When we look back at what was done to Jesus then we will understand the severity of following Christ all the way to the Cross. We will have a better understanding in the route that we ourselves must take and why we must take it. Believers take this route because it is the route to the Cross. Meaning, we as believers have to take our own route of Crucifixion to live the life that is pleasing in Gods site. Yes we must crucify the flesh so that we can live by the spirit. For if the flesh is not submissive to the spirit of Christ you find yourself doing things that are not like Christ. For example you might find yourselves worrying, fearing, cussing, fighting, smoking, drinking, and maybe even stealing. These are things that please the flesh and can or will cause you to fall away from God. That is why we must renew our mind and begin to crucify the flesh so that we can be free from the desires of sin.

However we can only do this when we make the decision to live completely and totally for Christ. When we begin to surrender our lives to Him and learn of Him we are crucified with Him. For truly this crucifixion of the flesh I speak of can be best explained in the entire book of Romans. Nevertheless I will just reference a small part to prove to the reader that it is not impossible. *"What shall we say then? Shall we continue in sin, that grace may abound? God forbid. How shall we, that are dead to sin, live any longer therein? Know ye not, that so many of us as were baptized into Jesus Christ were baptized into his death? Therefore we are buried with him by baptism into death: that like as Christ was raised up from the dead by the glory of the Father, even so we also should walk in newness of life. For if we have been planted together in the likeness of his death, we shall be also in the likeness of his resurrection: Knowing this, that our old man is crucified with him, that the body of sin might be destroyed, that henceforth we should not serve sin. For he that is dead is freed from sin. Now if we be dead with Christ, we believe that we shall also live with him." (Romans 6:1-8 KJV)*

Now after we crucify the flesh then you must be tried by a group of your peers. You would think that after all you went through to subdue your flesh that would be enough but *Oh No*. Here is where the real test comes when other people that you know, love, and care about begin to crucify you for the sake of Christ. They begin to lie on you just as they did Jesus. They begin to walk away from you, betray you, and say all manner of evil against you. They truly become an enemy of yours not because of anything you have done to them but because of who you have become in Christ. They truly nail your character and your emotions to a cross. Then you have to walk in a season of hurt and pain. You become confused as to what and why this happened unless you are spiritually mature enough to understand it on your first encounter. As you go on in your spiritual walk you realize that it was only a test and that trials are just a test of your faith. It doesn't change the fact that it caused you great distress but my question to you would be: Did you pass the test? SELAH.

For many of us in our surrendering to the Lord forgot one thing. We forgot to count the cost of following Christ.

Count the Cost

"And whosoever doth not bear his cross, and come after me, cannot be my disciple. For which of you, intending to build a tower, sitteth not down first, and counteth the cost, whether he have sufficient to finish it?"

(Luke 14:27-28 KJV)

What I will never understand in my spiritual walk was how I truly never thought to count the cost. This is why I choose (with of course the Lords help) to speak about this subject. I think because of lack of knowledge and spiritual immaturity I missed this concept. However it is never too late. When you become spiritually mature in your walk with the Lord you recognize that there is truly a cost to follow Christ and it is very expensive. Now when I talk about expensive not only does ministry cost you financially but it also cost you physically, emotionally, intellectually, and spiritually. It cost you physically because you have to take some invisible wounding that cause physical illness. The enemy (the devil) comes after your health. In my case it was through many miscarriages and complications from miscarriages that Satan tried to take my life. Though the enemy wasn't very successful at it because I am still living for God spared me from death. Then the devil tried to take my hearing and my mobility by making me cripple but once again God spared me. I couldn't understand why God would allow these things to happen but as time went on I realize there was a price to pay to follow Jesus.

Now that was some of the physical prices I had to pay though I am sure other believers paid different physical issues. Let us look at the emotional and social prices that we as Christians must pay. The most common one is walking away from your old lifestyle and friends who don't line up with Gods will for your life. Your social activities change from where you use to go to maybe a dance club, and maybe dance and enjoy some of the secular music with explicit language to going to church on Friday to prayer group and Bible study. Not only do you give it up for the sake of Christ but also you really don't desire to do these things anymore. You have sold out to your Christianity and now your likes and desires have changed. Let's not misinterpret what I am saying don't get fanatical about things. Let the Holy Spirit teach you and guide you into your social changes. In the midst of all of the personal changes try and help lead your friends and family to Christ. You never want to leave an opportunity to save a soul undone. For truly that is what this whole spiritual walk is about bringing souls to Christ for salvation.

That is what Satan doesn't want you to accomplish that is why the battle is so tough. The price we pay as saints and believers emotionally is even sometimes worst then physically and socially. Why? Because sometimes and maybe even ninety-nine percent of the time the emotional hurts comes from fellow believers and even your peers in the church. Yes as we look back even at Jesus life it wasn't His enemies that crucified Him it was the religious sector and the Jews who turned against Him. It was the Jews that were calling out to Crucify Him and let a criminal like Barabas go free. It is the same thing in the church today it is not the world that is tainting your spirit, lying on you, betraying you, or being hypocritical to you it is the church. It is supposedly the sold out believer who love Christ that is causing more chaos then the one who doesn't even know God. We as leaders, fivefold, sisters, and brothers are being hurt, mistreated, and abused by one another instead of being healed, delivered, and set free to walk in your purpose and destiny. It is a shame but if the God and the church told the truth it is real and very much alive right here in the Body of Christ.

So before you surrender your life to Christ remember to count the cost. Though the anointing and the spiritual walk is pricey it also worth it. For truly God payment is much greater than any payment man or the world could give you. For the word of the Lord simply says: *"The blessing of the Lord maketh rich and addeth no sorrow."* What God gives He doesn't take back nor does God discredit that which He called or ordained. Only mankind does that (discredits); for surely what God ordains He will maintain.

For now that we have counted the cost of your salvation now you must decide if you are willing to go forward and deny yourself.

Self-Denial

"Then said Jesus unto his disciples, If any man will come after me, let him deny himself, and take up his cross, and follow me."

(Matthew 16:24 KJV)

When you begin to count the cost of salvation and sanctification; one of the prices to pay is denying yourself and taking up the Cross of Christ. What does that mean? It basically means that your life is no longer your own it belongs to Christ. Everything you do or say is predicated on what God wants to do in your life. When you denial yourself you are refusing to comply with what you want or desire out of life. The request or petitions that you have for God have been change to the request that God has of you. To make quite plain and simple there are simply just some things that you have to give up during your lifetime for the sake of your destiny. Let me say this all of the things that you may have to sacrifice is not always bad. We can understand why we need to give up all of the bad habits and uncanny behavior. But how do you explain the good things that you must walk away from.

For example Abraham had to walk away from his family and his birthplace. It wasn't that it was so bad. However in order for God to do what He needed to do in Abraham's life He had to leave His comfort zone. Yes sometimes God test your faith and your love for Him by asking these hard requests. See because according to the word of God you must love God more than anything even your family. So God test your faithfulness to see if you will walk away from something or someone you love for the sake of the Cross. In order to be a true disciple of Christ you must deny yourself of everything that's not like Christ. You might have to deny your positions that you obtained in the world for the position God has preordained for you in the church. I have to finally give up my nursing job for full-time ministry. *"So likewise, whosoever he be of you that forsaketh not all that he hath, he cannot be my disciple."* (Luke 14:33 KJV)

You must walk away from the old life and enter into a new life with Christ. There is no getting around it. You must forsake all to get all Christ has for you. In life you can fool people and maybe even convince yourself that all is forsaken but you will never fool

Christ. He knows the truth but what I love about Christ is He always sends you help. Christ knows that denial of self is a hard process and it cannot be done without some divine help. Your help comes from the Holy Spirit. He gives you the knowledge, the wisdom, the power, and the strength to go through this hard process.

So as you begin to sanctify yourself and become obedient to the Lord, He begins to open some doors (opportunities & blessing) no man can shut and shut others doors (distractions & diversions) no man can open.

OPEN AND SHUT DOORS

"And to the angel of the church in Philadelphia write; These things saith he that is holy, he that is true, he that hath the key of David, he that openeth, and no man shutteth; and shutteth, and no man openeth; I know thy works: behold, I have set before thee an open door, and no man can shut it: for thou hast a little strength, and hast kept my word, and hast not denied my name."

(Rev 3:7-8 KJV)

See when you deny yourself, keep Gods word and have not denied His name, God will open doors for you that no man can shut. I never quite understood this scripture well until I had a few Christians shut some doors on me deliberately. Even though we know that God has the final say sometimes God will allow people to shut some doors of opportunities on you. Why does God allow this? Simply because He has to let you know that He is God and besides Him there is no other. Meaning that once this happens to you: you learn not to rely on people for anything but to trust God for everything. Yes sometimes the open and shut doors in your life are there to teach you valuable lessons. For God is so Sovereign that he will make your enemies or shall I say your assigned haters bless you. What's so great about it all is they (your enemies) don't even realize it. See anyone or anything that comes against Gods plan for your life is your enemy. It does not necessarily mean that people or circumstances are your enemies or haters. That is just what the devil uses to come against the people of God and Gods purpose and plan for your life.

You must be careful that as God opens and shuts doors (opportunities, blessings, and promises) for you that you don't become an enemy yourself. For every blessing and every opportunity that God gives us is truly so we can be a blessing to someone else. So when God opens a door of blessings for you through someone, you make sure you also do the same for the next person who deserves it. For I myself have had some doors shut in my face by leaders. However I did not get mad or bitter though I became discouraged and disappointed. Now I can see why God allowed it because what I thought was a blessing ahead was not what God had planned for my life. As one door closed God saw fit to open another one and take me into a new place and another dimension in ministry and writing. God opened up a door for me to meet a Publisher/Chief-Editor named Larry Montgomery who owned a Long Island paper called The Community Journal.

God truly has a sense of humor for it was at a dinner invitation that Mr. Montgomery offered me a trial opportunity to write an article for his paper. Who would have thought that a dinner invitation would turn into such an enormous blessing from God? That one dinner invitation turned into a weekly column in the Community Journal called "Life Changing Words" and a position as an Associate Editor of a new all Gospel magazines called "The Gospel News Journal". Now not only did that dinner open doors and stretch my faith in God but it pushed me to another level in ministry. For now my writing had become a ministry and not just a task or a one-time opportunity. I thank God for the divine connection that God has done between the Montgomery's and the Deadwyler's for we are not only Christians on assignment be we have truly become friends.

So let me say this don't be discouraged when the enemy closes a door on you but know that God has your feet prepared to walk in another direction.

Light Walking

"Then Jesus said unto them, Yet a little while is the light with you. Walk while ye have the light, lest darkness come upon you: for he that walketh in darkness knoweth not whither he goeth."

(John 12:35 KJV)

When God begins to shed some light on your purpose, plan,

and destiny let me say this: "He does not need any help". You must learn as a Christian how to walk in the light. Light walking means to walk according to Christ's will, ways, and statue. You must renew your mind for the path that you must take in your Christian walk. Not one person has the same plan from God for their life but we all have seasons of light and darkness. "Daniel answered and said, Blessed be the name of God for ever and ever: for wisdom and might are his: And he changeth the times and the seasons: he removeth kings, and setteth up kings: he giveth wisdom unto the wise, and knowledge to them that know understanding: He revealeth the deep and secret things: he knoweth what is in the darkness, and the light dwelleth with him." (Daniel 2:20-22 KJV)

There is an appointed time for you to walk in the light so that God can expose you and raise you up into who He ordained you to be. It is your responsibility as a Christian to recognize God's timing and hear His call. You must do many of your God-given assignments by faith and trust and believe God for the victorious outcome. Light walking takes much prayer, praise, and worship. In order to hear from God we will have to get in His presence. Getting in His presence can open the door to some hidden blessings and can also stir up some dormant gifts. For when we walk in the light it opens our eyes to many things in the natural and in the spiritual. First and foremost it lets God show you who He truly called you to be in the spirit. This in turn will shed some light on what is going on in your life in the natural. For example if He called you to be a millionaire then you find yourself naturally poor or in a financial bind. This can explain why it looks opposite of what God said but it will also help you to keep the faith. For when you were walking in the light God said you would be a millionaire and now a dark season has come in your finances. The enemy will try and tell you that what God said is a lie but you will remember or shall I say the Holy Spirit will bring back to your remembrance what God said to you during your light walking season.

It is in your darkest seasons that you can find God and build your faith. For when we are in the darkness we know not which way to go or to turn. So we must turn to the light, which is Jesus Christ. It is at this time in your life when you can understand the scripture "He is a lamp to my feet and a light to my path". You cannot see my way; you can't even see the path to which direction you need to go. But in your dark season if you can find Jesus, He will shed light on which direction you need to go and He will open up a path for you to find help in your times of trouble. He will make a way out of no way for truly He is the Way, the Truth, and the Life. For Gods plan is always for you to recognize that no matter where you find yourself at in this road called life, never forget He can change any and every situation. For when you walk in the light and have fellowship with Christ He will order your steps according to His word.

Ordered Steps

"Order my steps in thy word: and let not any iniquity have dominion over me."

(Psalms 119:133 KJV)

God is the only one that can order your steps in His word and keep you from having sin overtake you during your lifetime. He is the only one that knows you and your plan and His purpose for your life. He created you for a specific purpose and your life has value in the eyesight of God. He is your creator and He is the only one that knows the totality of your life. He can order your steps because He can see the beginning and He knows the end of your life. He also knows what is in between those two major points and how to protect you from the enemy's plan against your life.

See when God gives you a word for your life. He is the one who will orgistrate the plan so that the word can manifest itself in the natural. Whether it is a written word from the Bible or a spoken word from a prophet does not matter. What matters is that it is a true word from God and He is the one who will bring it to pass. Once the word is spoken it (the word) and you must be tried and tested by Satan. We never have to worry about Gods word failing because it is infallible. The only thing that can fail is our faith or a false prophetic word. That is why you must trust God to order your steps and not man. Though man may have good intentions for you it may not be Gods divine plan. So we must always make sure that it is not mans or our own desires that we are following.

For without the help of Christ we will walk in error and have to pay a price for it. The price hopefully will teach you to obey Christ and not yourself or others. Obedience to Christ can take you places that man can never take you. When Christ orders your steps there is only victory at the end of the tunnel. For as you begin to walk in the light and doors of opportunities start to manifest themselves you have no doubt in your mind that God did it. Things that you know you had no control of start to surface. Spiritual gifts and natural talents begin to get stirred up and you begin to perfect the things that God has placed in you. Even the hidden gifts or shall I say latent gifts start to manifest. You find yourself being lead into some things and areas of life that you never experienced. You find that you can lay hands on the sick and they recover. You learn that you have been baptized in the Holy Spirit and you can give true prophetic words and interpret tongue. You will find out that you have creative writing skills that you never knew existed and a mighty ministry to be birthed-out.

When you give in and surrender your life to God you find yourself walking right into destiny. You find out that Gods plan for your life is a little different than your plan. You realize that Gods plan is better and greater than you could ever think or imagine. When God orders your steps there is no failure even though there maybe some unexpected obstacles, situations, and circumstances. As Romans 8:28 say He works it all out for our good. For if we obey Gods ordered steps in our life then we shall prosper and be in health even as our soul prospers. If we don't obey God and become selfish we can fall into the hands of Satan and take the wrong route.

THE WRONG ROUTE

"There is a way that seemeth right unto a man, but the end thereof are the ways of death."

(Proverbs 16:25 KJV)

Now when we look at this scripture we must recognize that Satan is a deceiver. See in life there are ways that look and seem successful but in the end there is destruction. Our world system is one of those ways. If you do not recognize that there is a Savior to keep you from your destructive behavior your destiny will be hell. The world system really doesn't teach you about Christ and the Cross-. It is the church or shall I say the Body of Christ job to teach you about salvation and heaven as your destiny. Understand that I am not saying that all the world systems are wrong but what I am saying is that it is not eternal. When you die there is only two choices heaven or hell but that decision must be made while you are alive and living in the world.

The world teaches you good as well as bad things. It is up to you what you choose to follow. Will you follow the laws of the land or will you live by grace through faith in Christ. See the wrong route teaches you to be covetousness and selfishness. It makes you believe that life is about you and your wants and desires. Satan will encourage you to do things that please the flesh and your own selfish desires. He will make you believe that you are greater than you are and that life is all about you. As Christians you must be careful that the gifts, blessings, and talents that God gave you don't take you down the wrong road. You must make sure you don't get so caught up in all the drama and accolades that man give you that you miss God's purpose and become a castaway.

Don't Become a Castaway

> *"I therefore so run, not as uncertainly; so fight I, not as one that beateth the air: But I keep under my body, and bring it into subjection: lest that by any means, when I have preached to others, I myself should be a castaway."*
>
> *(1 Corinthians 9:26-27 KJV)*

Those of us who are Christians our lives are used daily to spread the Gospel. It doesn't matter whether we use our mouths to talk about the goodness of Jesus or our hands to help someone to overcome; we are considered the walking living examples and epistles of God. What do I mean by this? People watch everything that you do and listen to every word you say. Since they cannot see God in the natural (for God is a spirit) the only examples of Christ they see are those of us who call themselves Christians. So let us walk in the image of God through faith in His word and by the power of the Holy Spirit. When I say God's image we must clearly understand what that means. For we are to exhibit those characteristics of Christ am I saying that we are to be perfect like Him no for all of us fall short of the Glory of God?

No not one of us can ever become perfect but we continually

run the race of maturity that we may complete those things which God has given us to do. Which is just explaining that when you see a disciple of Christ striving to live for our Great and wonderful God don't judge him for his imperfections but help him to do right. See we all have some issues and problems that we have been dealing with during our lifetime and just because we have decided to live for Christ does not mean they have disappeared or that we have been healed or delivered as of yet. See sometimes the world believes that when you make the decision of *salvation* that you are blessed and made perfect but the opposite actually happens the enemy begins to challenge your faith and your progress. You find yourself fighting those things in your life that at one time were your crutches or your heart desires. Then finally when you think that you have conquered that, God begins to show you other areas in your life that He is not please with. Before you know it you have become a changed person and life has a different meaning and now you desire to work for the Kingdom of God and live to declare God's matchless and majestic Glory.

That's when you find yourself trying to live the word and be a doer of the word and not a hearer only. You begin to find out the indwelling Holy Spirit (living inside of you) has given you the power and authority to run this race (your Christian walk) with confidence and boldness. Now you know what your plans, purpose and destiny is from God and you're on a quest to fulfill it. You begin to teach, pray, or preach according to Gods will and ways not according to your own. And so you find the anointing is on your life and all that God has said to you is beginning to manifest itself in one form or another and you have become excited. Please I beg of you let not that excitement become pride but truly rely on God to bring your flesh under subjection. For if your carnal nature begins to raise its ugly head you are in danger of losing the race. After all you have done and all the time that you have put into ministry and purpose please for the sake of the Cross don't lose focus. Remember no matter how hard it gets and how impossible it may seem keep your focus on God. For your life has become a living testimony to all that know you and to whoever has been in your very presence. The world has watched you mature and go forth and have learned from those things that you have said, done, and lived; now after all this **"*Don't become a Castaway*"** yourself…

Now what is a castaway? According to the revelation of God it is someone who started the race correctly but somewhere along running the race or at the end of the race they became disqualified. For by the grace of God there goes I…remember stay focus and stay on course don't become rejected or make a shipwreck but run your race with endurance, honesty, and integrity so that in the end…You can hear the Father say **"Well done thy good and faithful servant come on HOME!!!!**

THE AUTHOR AND FINISHER

"Looking unto Jesus the author and finisher of our faith; who for the joy that was set before him endured the cross, despising the shame, and is set down at the right hand of the throne of God."

(Hebrews 12:2 KJV)

Now as we have read all of this chapter or various parts of this book we as Christians must understand that God is the Author and finisher of our faith. He is the one that made it all possible for us to run our race in Christianity. He was the first among many and we must set our eyes on the prize of heaven as our home. We must stay focused on what God has set before us and we must run the race with passion, persistence, and Gods endurance. We must rely solely on our faith and Christ strength to get us to the finish line. We must understand who Christ is and what we need from Him to be victorious. We need His word, His Spirit, His Blood, His Mind, and His tenacity.

We need all of this and more to endure the Cross-that is set before us. You must remember never to get caught up in your failures and never to get stuck in your pitfalls or dark seasons. As Christians you must use the Holy Spirit to help guide you and teach you to persevere even in the times of trouble or weakness. For the word of God simply says when we are weak Christ is strong. In all that we have endured through and will endure there must be a passion and zeal in us to push past the mess into our destiny just as Jesus did. Although he got weary in the flesh and fearful of the plan He never gave up or gave in. His exact words were: "Then saith he unto them, My soul is exceeding sorrowful, even unto death: tarry ye here, and watch with me. And he went a little farther, and fell on his face, and prayed, saying, O my Father, if it be possible, let this cup pass from me: nevertheless not as I will, but as thou wilt." (Matthew 26:38-39 KJV)

See Jesus knew that after all of the heartache, suffering, pain, and crucifixion there would be victory. So In reality He had a joy in His spirit to go to the Cross. Jesus knew the joy first and that made it easy to follow the plan because the plan was horrific but the joy of His victory was eternal. No we do not always like the road or the way we must take but we do know the end result with Christ is victory.

The Five Rights of this Christian walk is not always ideal but when you learn and experience them they shall and will become medication for your soul!

Chapter Seven

Medication for your Soul

As we enter into this last chapter I want you to know that these topics that I address are medication for your soul. Now that you have been through the five rights of spiritual life you realize that there are some things that you have learned from personal experience and from lack of knowledge. See the lack of knowledge can cause your spiritual death if you are not careful of the enemy's plot against you. It causes hurt and pain because you find yourself trusting people just because of their title and not paying attention to their character. Many Christian are walking around forever bruised and battered because of fellow saints, leaders, and pastors who have inflicted unnecessary but yet intentional pain on them. They have come across this false ideology that they are going to strengthen you for your spiritual destiny and instead they get pleasure in flexing their power and authority. They misuse what God has given them and they have lost sight of their purpose as leaders and fellow believers.

What I have found is that all of these experiences are to build your character, mature you in the faith, and teach you spiritual lessons. Your personal experiences will teach you what to do as a Christian and it will also teach you what not to do as a Christian. But the most important lesson of all is that no matter how bad it may seem or hurt Jesus has the power to heal you and turn all these afflictions around. It reminds me of the scripture the devil meant it for evil but God has turned it around for my good. So we must remember in all that we go through if we stay connected to Jesus and keep our minds focused on Him all of our afflictions will become medication for our soul. Meaning Jesus will not leave you bruised, battered, and broken but that He will use all of your experiences good and bad to mature you and heal you. Not only that: there is also a reward for the work that you have done.

> *"For the Son of man shall come in the glory of his Father with his angels; and then he shall reward every man according to his works."*
>
> (Matthew 16:27 KJV)

REWARDS FOR YOUR WORK

Yes many of us forget that Jesus shall reward our works on earth. Basically God is saying, "I am watching you". Every move you make and everything you do is being watched and judged by the Savior. A lot of times because God is not flesh we forget that He is omnipresent (everywhere at the same time), and omniscience (all-knowing). So when you do a work for the kingdom or against the Kingdom it has not gone unnoticed. You must recognize God rewards your work according to the state of your heart. Meaning if your motives are pure you will be blessed but if your motives are wrong you will be rebuked, chastised, or maybe even cursed.

Many of us are blessed because we have the heart of God. We are not out to compete with one another but our motives as Christians is to build one another up. Yes hurt and afflictions will come but thank God for the person that God sends to speak a healing into your life. See afflictions are necessary for us to learn Gods ways and become closer to God. From afflictions we learn to trust God for everything and be careful of mans intentions toward you. We must realize somebody is assigned to afflict you (and we will not give this person any credit) and somebody is assigned to heal you.

Learning by Afflictions

Psalms 119:71 KJV "It is good for me that I have been afflicted; that I might learn thy statutes."

As we walk through this road called *life* we are faced with various tests, trials, and tribulations, which leave us with pain and heartache. In the Bible God calls them afflictions. An affliction is a state of pain or distress; that which causes suffering, a calamity, or a misfortune. We as the Body of Christ face these issues daily. Every time we look around someone is being abused and mistreated right here in the Body of Christ. Yet we as Christians sit daily, weekly, monthly, and yearly in church without getting what Christ went to the Cross-for. Christ suffered and died at Calvary so you could be saved, healed, delivered, and set free.

An affliction changes your life but today I want to deal with how afflictions also change your thoughts. See when you have been afflicted or hurt sometimes it makes you think negative. This takes a toll on your emotions, and even sometimes your mental status. When your emotions become out of control your behavior follows. See if you're angry you respond incorrectly and maybe to abruptly and if you're oppressed you may not respond at all. Whichever way you lean in your thinking it will make the difference in how you see things and how quick you heal.

However thanks be to God that He has the power to change your mind and bring you back into right standing and thinking. For when you read the word of God, The Lord says, "It is good that we have been afflicted" but how in the world can we comprehend that it is good? See when we look back over our lives and think about all that the Lord Jesus has brought us through and to; we can then understand His kind of thinking. For if we had not been afflicted we would have never learned who He is.

We would have never known He was *Jehovah Rapha* our healer if we never got sick and /or afflicted. We would never have learned that He is *Jehovah Jireh* our provider if we never were broke. So although we never want to face sickness, diseases, hurt, betrayal, sufferings, hardships, and calamity throughout life we must understand that when we do there is reason for these things and it is to learn thy statures.

So I will impart this thought to you...***For if Jesus had not been afflicted where would we be....***

Thank the Lord for the person that God assigns to heal you for everybody will not risk himself or herself for your sake. I thank God that in the midst of my affliction God sent an Apostle to help me and explain to me why? What? And How? This person took time to explain to me the road to spiritual growth, ministry, and healing. Though others had the opportunity to do right they chose not to. Instead of trying to mend the situation they ignore it and made it worse. So I just had to take time to give a shout out to all obedient leaders that will obey God and not fall to peer and church pressure.

I give a special thanks to the one who took time to pray with me and speak healing into my life and I pray blessing upon you Apostle. I believe in giving credit where credit is due. May God reward you for the work you have done in me. This person made it easier for me to go on and not to in turn afflict those who walk with me. I have learned that if I inflict the pain, I must repent, apologize and make all things right in the eyesight of God. It is so important to get a true understanding of this spiritual walk and a healing in the midst of all your pain. It doesn't matter who hurt you what matters is that you learn Jesus can heal you. Now how Jesus does it is solely up to Him!

What I will say though is when I look back at the situation although it may not make sense to many people the "Hurt was worth it"...

Hurt is Worth

"And they departed from the presence of the council, rejoicing that they were counted worthy to suffer shame for his name. And daily in the temple, and in every house, they ceased not to teach and preach Jesus Christ."

(Acts 5:41-42 KJV)

"For I reckon that the sufferings of this present time are not worthy to be compared with the glory which shall be revealed in us."

(Romans 8:18 KJV)

We all know that pain and suffering is a part of life. As we go through this life, situations and circumstances comes to test our faith in God. What I have learned in the midst of my suffering is that the hurt that has been afflicted on me has been worth it. See when I look back over my life I realized that it (my sickness, betrayal, pain, and suffering) caused my spiritual growth. Had I not had a battle with miscarriages, loss of blood, and impending death, I would not have the relationship with God that I have. These unfortunate circumstances in my life caused me to look, lean, and depend on God.

The doctors could not save me for it was through their mistakes and errors that I almost died. Thank God that God saw fit to send the warring angels on my behalf and His word that said you will live and not die to declare the Glory of God. As I went through all of this I learned how to pray and press my way through my physical problems by using my spiritual weapons. It was through my hurt I received full revelation of Jesus suffering on the Cross-for me. I understood that He would be the first among many to suffer and die because of righteousness. However what Satan did not know was that Jesus would rise again in three days. In Jesus rising I learned that I could also rise. Not as Jesus did in the resurrection but that through Him I could spiritually and physically rise from this incident and occurrence in my life. Though the doctors were negligent thank God Jesus blood was permanent. For before I even got in this situation Jesus Blood had already covered me. So when the enemy seen the Blood, though Satan may not have liked it, Satan had no choice he had to pass over me.

It is no different for any other Christian that has been attacked, abused, misused, or mistreated. Yes the weapons will form against you but one thing I am sure of is they will not prosper. Yes people will and shall lie on you, treat you bad, and even hurt you but one thing I like about Jesus is He will redeem you. When it is happening we cannot see the full value or manifestation of what God is doing in our life. We just are focused on the flesh and the unfair treatment but when you look pass the immediate actions into the future you realize it was all for your good. Sometimes it was done so you could learn from life's experiences other times it was done because God wanted to expose a situation or maybe even a person. For whatever reason that it was done God has the solution to your hurt and also to your worth. See we found out that as sinners we were (in Christ mind) worth dying for. See the love that He had for us caused Him to look past who we were and see who we were called to be.

We were called to be heirs to the throne, royal priesthood, and a peculiar people. We were called to walk in the light and be the light to a dark world. We were called to be ministers of the Gospel and proclaim Christ work on the Cross. This in turn also makes us targets to Satan and his demonic forces. When we become targets we get in the line of fire and our faith is tested. We may never be able to explain all of the suffering that a person may go through in life but it will never be compared to what Christ went through. So just as Christ overcame Satan and victory was the end result we can overcome the enemy as well. According to Revelation 12:11 *"And they overcame him by the blood of the Lamb and by the word of their testimony; and they loved not their lives unto the death."*

So thank God for your hurt and healing for you have been persecuted for righteousness sake.

Persecuted for Righteousness Sake

"Blessed are they which are persecuted for righteousness' sake: for theirs is the kingdom of heaven. Blessed are ye, when men shall revile you, and persecute you, and shall say all manner of

evil against you falsely, for my sake. Rejoice, and be exceeding glad: for great is your reward in heaven: for so persecuted they the prophets which were before you."

(Matthew 5:10-12 KJV)

When you are persecuted for righteousness sake it is a blessing in disguise. I know that does not make sense to the carnal mind but according to the word of God it is true. These are the lessons we learn as we mature and perfect our faith. You will learn not to take everything that is falsely said against you personal and also that it is the devils job to persecute you for living a righteous life through Christ. This is one of the hardest experiences to walk through because you just never expect a believer to persecute you for doing what is right. Especially considering they are suppose to be helping you and supporting you but yet you find them intentionally trying to destroy you. The first time that happen to me it blew my mind for I just couldn't comprehend it in the natural.

Why would a person who lives for the Lord want to do something so horrific as that? Then I remembered what Jesus went through and I begin to understand this a little better. Once I realized it was not about me but it was about the Christ that lives in me. I begin to rejoice and be exceedingly glad for truly my reward shall be great. My reward is not contingent on what people do to me but what I do to people even when they are wrong. So let not any men strip you of your name or your integrity. For both are precious commodities to God.

Integrity and Trust

"The integrity of the upright shall guide them: but the perverseness of transgressors shall destroy them."

(Proverbs11: 3 KJV)

"O keep my soul, and deliver me: let me not be ashamed; for I put my trust in thee. Let integrity and uprightness preserve me; for I wait on thee."

(Psalms 25:20-21 KJV)

One thing that I have learned in this spiritual walk is that integrity and trust is a key factor to your character. You as a Christian must have integrity in everything you do. You may never please man but one thing for sure if you please God you will walk in integrity and people will trust you with their lives as well as their souls. See as we are closing in this last chapter of this book we are talking about medication for your soul and if your character lines up with God's word it is like medicine to your soul. One thing we must all learn is no matter how hurt or discouraged you become you must never become vengeful. Not even when people have spoken all matter of evil against you and even attempted to come against your character and assignment from God. You must be steadfast and unmovable meaning you should not be easily emotionally affected. But to have peace at night while you are sleeping and obtain Gods glory in our lives we must always try with the help of Christ to do the right thing no matter what.

Do the Right Thing

"Withhold not good from them to whom it is due, when it is in the power of thine hand to do it. Say not unto thy neighbour, Go, and come again, and to morrow I will give; when thou hast it by thee."

(Proverbs 3:27-28 KJV)

Many times we as leaders, parents, and maybe even young teenagers come across situation and circumstances that are left in our hands where we have to make a choice. However in this hour and time where there is so much sin running ramped in the world God is still looking for a few saints who are willing to "Do the Right Thing."

No matter what opposition comes against you and how hard it may get we as Christians as well as good moral citizens should never withhold from anyone what is due to them. Lots of times as you walk through life you see people treated unfairly because of their color, creed, age, religion, financial status and their outward appearance. We assume because they have it all together (or at least it seems like it) that they don't need another blessing or great opportunity from God. However that is not our call or place to decide that for if it is due to them then we must not tarry with their blessing. Neither should we deny them of it because of our personal opinions or assumptions.

We must learn how not to abuse our power or positions as we

grow in natural and spiritual wisdom. For what we must realize is if we deny them we deny ourselves as well. You must understand that God blesses those who walk upright and do good because when you do this you exhibit His very nature and walk in His image. This in turn is pleasing in His sight. What I have learned in my walk with the Lord is that "If you take care of The Father's (GOD'S) business, He will take care of yours."

So when your test comes to do good for others don't fail it because of personal issues but through faith in God "Do the Right Thing." For truly if we do the right thing "the LORD will give us His grace and glory and surely no good thing will he withhold from us that walk upright." This is also a sign of spiritual maturity for the believer.

Spiritual Maturity vs. Spiritual Immaturity

"Now the God of peace, that brought again from the dead our Lord Jesus, that great shepherd of the sheep, through the blood of the everlasting covenant, Make you perfect in every good work to do his will, working in you that which is wellpleasing in his sight, through Jesus Christ; to whom be glory for ever and ever. Amen."

(Hebrews 13:20-21 KJV)

Spiritual maturity comes with experience and a relationship with God. You will never become spiritually mature if you do not seek God for wisdom, knowledge, and understanding. See because when you begin to mature in the things of God you no longer depend on your flesh but you begin to depend of your spirit. What do I mean by that? You begin to trust the spirit of the Living God that lives inside you to lead you and guide you into all truth. When you lean and trust in the Lord for the work that He has put before you it will take a maturing of your faith to perform it. It will not be done by your strength or your ability but all things will get done according to Gods will and His Spirit. Spiritual immaturity believes in self but spiritual maturity relies on the Holy Spirit. So as you perfect (mature) in the faith you recognize that it is more advantageous for all involved if you do it (whatever Gods work and will is for your life) by the spirit.

DOING IT BY THE SPIRIT

"Then he answered and spake unto me, saying, This is the word of the LORD unto Zerubbabel, saying, Not by might, nor by power, but by my spirit, saith the LORD of hosts."
(Zechariah 4:6 KJV)

When you think about the plans that you have for your life; are they really the same as what God has? We start out with plans that we desire and then we put it into effect trying to use our own strength and knowledge to do it. Thinking that our natural wisdom and knowledge will get us where we are trying to go. Surely there is nothing that we can do to change Gods plans for our life except to say "not my will but let Gods will be done in my life." Many things that we do are according to our own will and desires and there is nothing wrong with it. We must take time out to plan and work on our lives but we must always realize that God is in control of the outcome.

Everything that we do is subject to the living Gods approval. Even when we use our knowledge to advance our lifestyles and change our circumstances; we still must understand that God is working in the midst of it all. Some things that we do are strictly subject to Gods Spirit of approval. In the midst of all that we do and accomplish in life there is still no question of who is in charge. Our accomplishments and goals that we obtained were strictly subject to the hand of God whether we were successful in it or not. God has situations, circumstances, and goals for us that we just don't have the ability to do, get out of or change but solely God will do it. We need him to intercede on our behalf and when He does it is accomplished through our prayers, faith, and His spirit.

Let me try to explain it this way: Have you ever been in a situation or circumstance that you know that if God does not do this for me it cannot be done. When you know that God has stepped in and performed a miracle in your life or given you something that you were not capable to obtain yourself you become thankful. For surely you did not have the knowledge, the wisdom, or the connections but what you failed to realize is that you had the most important ingredient that anyone could have. You had God!!!

So my word to you is there are some blessings in your life that are not coming by your might (strength), nor by your power (your authority or ability) but it is going to be done solely by the Spirit of the Living God. And when God does it nothing and no one has the ability to stop it, not even you....For He is truly "Doing it by the Spirit."

Now after you have learned how to do it by the spirit there comes another realization. That realization is that with God all things are possible. So even when man says no if God says yes then the answer is Yes!

WHEN GOD SAYS "YES"

"But Jesus beheld them, and said unto them, with men this is impossible; but with God all things are possible."
(Matthew 19:26 KJV)

When God says "Yes" there is nothing anyone can do or say to stop what He has ordained. For when God speaks surely it has to come to pass in the natural. So whatever God has promised you in this year or in the future don't be dismayed if you have not seen the manifestations of your promises yet. For God have an appointed time and the appointed day to show up and show out. What we must learn how to do is wait on God and have patience. Though God never does it like you expect Him to He will always keep His word. As a Christian I have truly learned His ways are not my ways neither are His thoughts my thoughts but surely God has a different way of doing things. Most of the time until full manifestation is completed it never makes sense to our natural or carnal mind.

Just when you think you have figured God out (smile) He makes a u-turn and does something completely the opposite of what you thought. That's why as Christians we have to learn to trust God and lean not on our own understanding but acknowledge Him in all our ways and He shall direct our path. Gods' path of righteousness is definitely a path that we as believers want to say yes to. His path for our life is so much greater than the path we could ever take or imagine for ourselves. Not only do we want God to say *Yes* but we must also surrender and say yes to God's will. That is when God can do the miraculous in our life, for to surrender to God is to open the door to the impossible.

In these days of uncertainty with the world, we all ought to be absolutely certain of God. Simply meaning that there is nothing impossible or too hard for God; so whatever you need from God is available through His Son all you have to do is ask for it. Just because you don't have enough money, knowledge, connections, or confidence to do what God called you to do, doesn't mean God can't do it. So don't give up or be dismayed but be encouraged and trust God. That is what faith is all about trusting God when you can't see, or understand but your hope is in the Almighty One.

So as you make your future plans to prosper never forget to leave the door open for God to bless your visions, hopes, and dreams. Why should you leave the door open? Because "Jesus beheld them, and said unto them, with men this is impossible; but with God all things are possible."

TAKE IT BY FORCE

"And from the days of John the Baptist until now the kingdom of heaven suffereth violence, and the violent take it by force."

(Matthew 11:12 KJV)

See what I love about God is that after He shows you nothing is impossible for Him. He teaches you that there are some things in this life and in your spiritual walk you will have to take by force. This means you must get aggressive in your spiritual walk and take some things back by force that the devil stole from you. You must use your spiritual weapons to defeat the enemy and not be a wimpy Christian. You must learn how to war in the spirit so that you can walk in victory and not become a victim of your circumstances.

WARRING IN THE SPIRIT

"For though we walk in the flesh, we do not war after the flesh: (For the weapons of our warfare are not carnal, but mighty through God to the pulling down of strong holds;) Casting down imaginations, and every high thing that exalteth itself against the knowledge of God, and bringing into captivity every thought to the obedience of Christ."

(2 Corinthians 10:3-5 KJV)

Life has a way of teaching us the error of our ways. As a mature Christian I learned that your fight is not with the people of the world but with the enemy of God, which is Satan. When you begin to go through your spiritual walk your wisdom, knowledge, and understanding of God becomes enlightened. We start to realize that our battle is not with our failures, depression, our oppression or ourselves but it is with the devil. These are the very things that the devil tries to use against you to keep you from obtaining the blessings God has for you. See you must understand that you are in a battle or shall I say a War.

Now when you think about being in a war there are two opponents for us one is the flesh or carnal nature and the other is God working through the person of the Holy Spirit. However unlike most wars we as Christians start out with the victory but the problem with that is most of us don't know that. So we spend our times fighting the enemy in the flesh instead of realizing that Jesus already conquered the enemy at the Cross. See we must look back at the Cross experience to understand our fight is not among one another. Since the beginning of mans *"Fall"* there has been enmity between Gods' creation (man) and the devil. What we need to comprehend is that if we would follow the commands of God, which is to be not conformed to this world but be ye transformed by the renewing of your mind, we could avoid a lot of the heartache and misery that we go through. Next if we could learn to put on the whole armor of God so that we would not be so vulnerable but we would be able to stand against the wiles (tricks and schemes) of the devil.

And last but not least we have to cast down imaginations that are contrary to the word of God and pull down all the strongholds (areas where Satan has you bound) that are truly holding you back from all the wonderful promises and blessing that God has specifically for you. So my word to you is do not let your flesh or Satan steal your future but fight (war) for what is rightfully yours through Christ the Lord....

My Merry Heart

"A merry heart doeth good like a medicine: but a broken spirit drieth the bones."

(Proverbs 17:22 KJV)

Though a broken vessel is what God can use in ministry you must understand that you cannot stay broken. A broken spirit drieth your bones simply speaking means it makes you bitter, angry, and vengeful. This is not what the Lord has in mind for a Christian and if you have any doubt about what I just said think about this. Jesus body and flesh was bruised and broken but they never broke His spirit. Why? Because he had to be a living testimony to us that though they slay me yet will I trust God. So when I look back on all I have been through (good and bad). I can honestly say that these trials and tribulations taught me how to trust God for all things. I now know to put my trust in God and not in people or shall I say man. For it is when we trust in God our hearts can be healed and become merry (joyous) and doeth the Kingdom of God good as we can become medicine to someone else soul.

Medication to my Soul

"But as for you, ye thought evil against me; but God meant it unto good, to bring to pass, as it is this day, to save much people alive."

(Genesis 50:20 KJV)

Now here is what I love about the great God that I serve. While I was going through all of my five rights God never gave me understanding of what He was doing in and through my life. I could not comprehend why I had gone through a lot of which seem to me unnecessary trials, hurts, rejections, persecutions, and betrayal. I realize now that it was truly to help others so they do not have to take the route I took and receive the wrong medication. When I look back over some of my spiritual and natural encounters I notice that at times I was either in the wrong place, with the wrong person, in the wrong timing, getting the wrong medication because somehow I had taken the wrong route. Taking the wrong route and/or medication can cause all sorts of issues in your life but remaining faithful and submitted to God will bring you out of it all. See God is faithful even when we are not. Even in the midst of continual prayer, reading, and studying the word of God, and fasting somehow I had either missed Gods voice or it was just my destiny so I could write this book.

Whatever the reason may be it takes me back to the scripture what the enemy meant for my evil God turned it around not only for my good but also for the good of anyone who will read this book. If you read this book and get true revelation knowledge you will be able to avoid some of the unnecessary things that I myself went through. You will be able to identify the wrong person because if their motive is not to help, teach, train, and love you then it is the wrong person to connect with. Just as well if you are in a place where you are not growing spiritually and being abused or misused then you are in the wrong place. At no time in your spiritual walk should you be abused or mistreated by the church or your spiritual leaders. Yes it does happen but it is not godly. For there is no place in the Bible where I have ever seen Jesus mistreat anyone to teach them a lesson but He did all things in love and that is what we as Christians should do. Now that I have informed the Christians of some of the wrongs let me show you in a quick synopsis how God reverse it and made it right.

> *"And he shall be like a tree planted by the rivers of water, that bringeth forth his fruit in his season; his leaf also shall not wither; and whatsoever he doeth shall prosper."*
>
> *(Psalms 1:3 KJV)*

After God finishes pruning you and putting you through the process He changes your direction. Which takes me to this great verse, which represents one of the end results of the process? We become like a tree planted by the river and everything we do begins to prosper. In my case God began to bring me into the knowledge of who I was and what I was called in the Kingdom to do. Then He started making room for my gift according to Proverbs 18:16 KJV: "A man's gift maketh room for him, and bringeth him before great men." Before I knew it I was in a place in God that I had never been, doing things I had never done with people who were for me and not against me. God had begun to open doors that no man could shut and close doors that no man could open. As God was shutting down those things that were not beneficial or good for me He was redeeming me from all of the lies and persecution.

It was now my season to be that tree and for God to prove Himself according to His word and promises. He divinely connected me to new people and a new covering and mentor was established over my ministry and over my spiritual life. This was truly a divine connection because my new spiritual mentor knew me (in the spirit realm first) and understood the plans that God had for my life. There was no envy, strife, jealousy, or confusion. It was all God and nothing that either one of us did could have changed what God had already done. Not only did God establish me spiritually as an Apostle, Prophetess, and Pastor but He also established me as a writer, columnist, and as an Associate Editor of the Gospel News Journal. Though there are many promises God has still to manifest He certainly put me back on the right route and now I am receiving the right medication, in the right timing of God, and being spiritually led by the right person. How do I know that? Because God took me to the water, planted me, and began to fulfill His word.

Planted by the Water

This is literally a true story about being planted by the water. This is where God chose to spiritually and physically heal, deliver, and set me free from all of the wrong medication. I went to Port St. Lucie, Florida for a women's conference and at the end of the conference several of us went to the beach. I was the new kid on the block and so I did not quite understand the whole concept of going to the water. However after we arrived there and God met us there it all begin to make sense. God first of all brought back to my remembrance His promises and His purpose for my life. Then He began to speak to me prophetically through the Apostles that were there. There were five Apostles there beside myself Chief Apostle Wallace, Chief Apostle Edrington, Jr. Chief Apostle McKnight (my covering), Apostle Hill, and Apostle Trollinger. So I knew right there God was giving me grace for the journey that was ahead of me and now it was time to change the wrong to right and wash away some of the old and instill something new.

As we stood on the beach on the shoreline the water started to come up on us. First we entered in by two's praying and holding hands as God did His cleansing and blessing individually and then we began to all hold hands and corporately pray. Not realizing that every time the waves came up they were washing, cleansing, healing, delivering, and imparting to all of us at the same time. God has a unique way of freeing His servants from the world and the mess in this case He used the water. Water truly represented the Holy Spirit as He used it the water became a typology of Christ death. We were baptized and as the water kept coming we kept sinking deeper and deeper into the sand until we were planted by the water and when Christ released us we became trees of righteousness. Our sins went down in the water and we rose with righteousness and power. We were now ready for our new journey because we had been cleansed, healed, renewed, restored, and revived by the Savior and the Holy Spirit.

So once again God had proved Himself faithful in Florida at the shore. God had brought us all to the right place to receive the right medicine (which was the Holy Spirit), to eradicate all the wrong that had taken place in our life. After eradicating the wrong He imputes all that is right. So now we have arrived at the place of which I call a ***Kairos*** moment; where time, purpose, and destiny just met because all of the five rights are in place….

**It is finished for I am established… and you
now have the right to the tree of life.
Come and Let's enter in!!!**

"And, behold, I come quickly; and my reward is with me, to give every man according as his work shall be. I am Alpha and Omega, the beginning and the end, the first and the last. Blessed are they that do his commandments that they may have right to the tree of life, and may enter in through the gates into the city."

(Revelation 22:12-14 KJV)

For as I close this book I also close the chapter on the last eight years of my life. I shall relinquish all the past hurts and pains, the betrayal that I went through by the law and my Judas as well as the Pharisees, Sanhedrin's, and Sadducees that I have encountered in my spiritual walk. However in the midst of it all, the writing of this very book has indeed become **medication to my soul** and I thank the Lord for using me, healing me, and completing me in this season….and establishing a new beginning in my life.

*B*IBLIOGRAPHY

Thorndike Barnhart Advanced Dictionary, 2nd ed. Glenview, IL: Scott Foresman, 1974.

www.ingramcontent.com/pod-product-compliance
Lightning Source LLC
Chambersburg PA
CBHW072336300426
44109CB00042B/1642